WIDOWHOOD
101
NEXT STEPS

A handbook to help newly widowed seniors
navigate this next phase of their lives....

Berenice E. Kleiman

Widowhood 101: Next Steps / Berenice E. Kleiman

ISBN: 9798579140258

Cover Design by Berge Design

Printed in the United States of America

Berenice@BereniceKleiman.com

Dedicated to the Memory of Herb Kleiman

Photo Credit to Norman Becker

Also by Berenice Kleiman:

One Stroke, Two Survivors
Lessons Learned: Stroke Recovery from a Caregiver's Perspective
Life is the Sum of My Choices

CONTENTS

CHAPTER I

PREFACE

WIDOWHOOD 101: NEXT STEPS offers a pragmatic guide for survival based on my own recent experience as a new widow in early April '20. I found my immediate financial situation so shocking that I'm determined to give a heads up to others who face this cataclysmic event.

Although I thought I was prepared and held updated wills and powers of attorney in hand, along with a comprehensive file of end-of-life plans, I immediately faced an onslaught of unexpected demands for esoteric information needed to establish my husband's loss and my identity. During the time it took to locate and provide this new information my funds became frozen and even my husband's pension and insurances were blocked. Many of these changes result from newly instituted legislative adjustments combined with the Coronavirus epidemic, and are more than likely to become permanent.

For example, I had no advance warning that I would need both my husband's and my birth certificates, our original social security cards, and even our original wedding license. Although I obviously thought I knew I would need and immediately applied for Herb's death certificate for applications for insurances and Social Security, even that remained beyond reach for almost two months.

These special certifications, all original, now replace the ubiquitous Social Security number recently removed from Medicare cards and drivers' licenses in compliance with new federal and state laws. And complicating an already difficult situation, Covid-19 forced closures of banks and government offices, and even access to churches, funeral chapels, synagogues, and bereavement groups. With this barrage of new demands and closed doors, my world lurched to a full stop, complicating my own grieving.

I hope the lessons I've learned under duress will help prepare new widows and widowers to more readily satisfy these intractable, new, and sometimes illogical identity pressures that create increasing mounds of immediate paperwork. Still, to put these issues in context, you're going to first learn a lot about me, my own devastating emotional loss, and my complicated steps to survival that have set the stage for the many lessons that conclude each chapter.

I hadn't initially expected to air my heartbreak like so many of the other "widow" books, but context is basic to explaining the fury I felt as these waves of unexpected demands swept over me. It made me curious about how others are faring under similar, immediate loss. I extensively draw upon interviews with friends and friends of friends, all of whom have lost spouses within the past decade. Although many of our issues overlap, I am one of the few I know now caught in this current pandemic.

The score of widows and widowers I've interviewed, while not statistically relevant, are friends within the age range from 65 to 80+. All have lost a spouse following a long, successful marriage, as marriages go, retain comfortable finances, have grown children, and are retired. This is also the same audience I hope to target with this book.

Overall, my queries mainly centered about how they've absorbed their losses. In long conversations, we focused on the economic, legal and social demands each encountered while struggling through their own grieving and recovery. Which demands surprised them the most? Even more broadly, what advice do they offer to those of us currently suffering from loss to survive and move on to next steps?

WIDOWHOOD 101: NEXT STEPS follows a pattern much like the two books about massive stroke I've previously written that were published by the Cleveland Clinic. Each chapter concludes with practical survival steps, some admittedly drawn from other materials, and many discovered on my own. I've used this collaborative advice to push forward through my loss, grieving, boredom and monotony, all with the goal of helping to make it easier for you as well.

Aging and loss have never been easy. In other cultures, some within far distant memory, the treatment for spousal survivors was severe. Asian Indian women were burned on the funeral pyre along with their dead (usually aged) spouses. That obviously eliminated the family problem for further caring and support. Innuits (read in the encyclopedias as

Eskimos before pc) had a less heated method of disposal. They set the ancient widow or widower (non-discriminatory) far out on an iceberg or on a solitary boat without a paddle. Sometimes, as an alternative, whole communities disappeared at night and moved on while the person in question was sleeping. In Biblical days, groups simply married the widow off to the next in the paternal line, whether spousal father, uncle, or a living brother-in-law.

Here in western culture, the way of bereavement seems to purposely distract and overwhelm the mourner with mounds of paperwork. Without laboring through this morass, how otherwise can we even begin to reclaim all the finances we thought were ours before the loss of our mate?

CHAPTER II

SAYING GOODBYE

I knew Herb was going to die. That came as no surprise because we'd fought together to sustain and provide his quality of life for almost 20 years since his massive stroke. Herb and I were tough and we didn't give up easily. From the beginning I promised him that although life in a wheelchair wouldn't be as good as before, he and I would still be better off than most people in our age range. My only request was that he fight along with me. Herb was 67 and I 63 when his right-sided stroke came as a bolt of lightning. Fortunately, for both of us, he was already on Medicare and backed by an excellent healthcare supplement.

Theatre buffs, we'd been at the Shaw Festival, in Niagara-on-the-Lake, Ontario, staying at a bed and breakfast when, on the morning of July 14, July 2001, he slurred his words. Immediately recognizing these stroke symptoms, I packed him up, paid the B&B lady, slammed a couple of aspirin in his mouth, and headed home to Cleveland driving 90 miles an hour. It was a Saturday morning and we were moving against traffic. I had every confidence, even crossing the Peace Bridge and customs, we could make it home within the three and a half-hour window to get a tPA[1] injection from the Cleveland Clinic to break up the clot(s) in his brain. Unfortunately, Herb chose not to tell me his terrible headache had begun the night before.

When I began writing our first book ONE STROKE, TWO SURVIVORS, Herb, my marketing guru and business partner, asked me "Who's your audience? Who's going to read this book?" He questioned whether this and our subsequent book (LESSONS LEARNED: STROKE RECOVERY FROM A CAREGIVER'S PERSPECTIVE) would be targeted to spousal caregivers and stroke

---

1   An IV injection, considered the gold standard treatment for isch-emic stroke, is usually given through a vein in the arm within the first 3.5 hours after the start of stroke symptoms to open up blood clots in the brain.

survivors. Both books hit our target because they offered something not previously done: we presented both our perspectives in separate fonts. Rather than relying on the clinical and personal themes in many of the books previously written, including strokes of luck, God and poetry, our books focused on our pragmatic survival experiences with tactics we discovered on our own.

Even without Herb I'm still following his guidance. Each chapter of WIDOWHOOD 101: NEXT STEPS concludes with Lessons Learned, as well as basic tips to fight system and social inertia that will help readers deal with loss and move on. Unlike many of the random handouts distributed by hospices and funeral services, these tips are matched to real needs and experiences.

As aging seniors, we deserve attention because there are so many of us. According to the most immediate reference, the "2017 U.S. Government Profile of Older Americans,"[2] our numbers are significant: 33% of older women or 9.3 million women, and 4.5 million men are widowed. And almost half of those living alone (45%) are aged 75 and over. Obviously, we represent a significant and growing cluster.[3] And we're not going to allow ourselves to be cast aside or moored on an iceberg.

Looking Backward

Herb and I did pretty well for most of those stroke years. Our son Steve tore our three-story, non-accessible Shaker Heights home apart, removed almost all doors, and moved Herb's computer and desk up from our joint basement office to the living room. We installed a chairlift, purchased five wheelchairs (upstairs, downstairs, garage, car trunk and a replacement) along with any and all other necessary equipment. Physical therapy became a must for all 19+ years.

We frequently traveled by car and plane, continued our passion for Stratford and Shaw Theatres, in Canada, took classes in nearby

---

2   Sources: U.S. Census Bureau, American Community Survey; Current Population Survey, Annual Social and Economic Supplement 1967 to present.

3   Looking at this from a different dimension: Because we live longer, women are more likely than men to lose a spouse. Roughly 34% of women 65 and older were widows in 2016, compared to about 12% of men. (Census Bureau)

colleges, and enjoyed travel to Turks & Caicos and Cancun, as well as local theatres, restaurants, and other activities here in Cleveland. With the help of a really good team of physicians in Cleveland and Baltimore, nurses and therapists, and special, part time aides, we managed to surmount most of the worst complications.

Life was pretty good until the last three years when Herb caught cold from a therapist at our therapy center. His cold developed into pneumonia and morphed into a continuing series of urinary tract infections. Walking with his pyramid side walker became more difficult and the complications cascaded into stays in emergency rooms, hospitals, and skilled nursing facilities. Based on the number of errors I witnessed, I rarely left Herb alone in these medical facilities and often shared nights by his bed sprawled across two chairs or on a recliner.

By September, 2019, Herb said he'd had enough and was ready to call it a day. After repeatedly falling out of our kingsize bed he was now in a separate room with a hospital bed and he hated his permanent catheter. His good left leg wasn't moving, which made it harder to transfer him to the downstairs recliner or even into the car. We required increasing assistance over multiple hours each day that extended into full-time, round-the-clock support during the last seven months. Recognizing our need, one of our aides offered to form her own nursing service and brought on board a team of well-chosen ladies who used an upstairs sitting room as their hub. That Herb would remain at home rather than in a nursing home was never in question. I promised him that he would be surrounded with love and care and die as comfortably as I and my team could make it. He did.

In the midst of this decline, I decided to submit an article that I thought would fit the format of the popular NEW YORK TIMES' "Modern Love" podcast. Saying goodbye to this man whom I'd loved so fully over so many decades needed to be expressed and shared. Death was not coming as a surprise for either of us. I thought that by talking openly, and lifting the kimono, I could hopefully make this transition easier rather than morbid. As with many of my other writings, I read the completed draft to Herb. THE NEW YORK TIMES wasn't excited about my submission but at least the writing helped me collect and express my thoughts.

How Do You Say Goodbye?

I look down on my sleeping husband. His face is relaxed. I take his curled hand and then bend and kiss him. It's not easy to say goodbye, even on slow time when you don't know whether you have days, weeks, even months. Saying goodbye is a slow process. I lay awake at night remembering those early years, some good, some not, but the balance worth repeating if there were still time. Over the years I've begged, maybe even convinced Herb to stay with me so we could grow old together. We kept our promise until we couldn't keep it any longer. The big king-size bed is even bigger now that one side is empty. Sometimes in the middle of the night I reach over to this nothingness. Sometimes the cat is there but most of the time the space is empty with no hand to reach out and take mine. After 56 years I really don't know how to sleep alone. Or wake up alone. Or even reconnect so that we stay joined in body and spirit.

Now when I look down on him in his hospital bed with railings up on both sides, I see flashes of the young man I fell in love with and have consistently loved through so many years. He was brash, hardheaded sometimes, and filled with dreams, ambitions and passion. During the first decade when I chose to remain at home raising our family, I used to watch him dress in the morning after his shower, meticulously put on his suit, tie, and give his shoes a final brush. It used to be fun to see if I could entice him to come back to bed with me, just a little while longer. Sometimes I won and the conquest was sparkling. But I also knew when to let go and look forward to the next evening. And the next. Still there were times when passion turned to dislike, back-to-back, no words between. The same energy that went into loving could turn with provocation. Making up, when the time came, was also glorious. I used to say, "I will always love you, but not always like you." And I really meant it.

I married someone who thought of himself (and I agreed) as controlling. But I was my own person, independent and not easily controlled or molded. We were both in our mid-twenties when we met and married. There had been other experiences that neither of us dwelled on. We basically knew ourselves, who we were and what we wanted. And we moved quickly: engaged in three months and married in seven. No point hanging around. We knew we'd each found our soulmate. We matched in background, temperament, intelligence, education, ambition, and hopes for the future. Others who knew us and our competitive spirits worried openly that we'd kill one another within two weeks. Herb was also the poorest fellow I'd ever dated. But somehow, I knew that we would work together in partnership through life for whatever we wanted. And we did. Our values and culture were similar. We shared interests and introduced one another to new ones that we also shared.

The beginning was choppy, just as others had predicted, because we battled for personal space in a relationship that could easily become stifling. Herb earned his doctorate at night while working full time. And I worked to support his dreams. Surprisingly for us, our family came quickly, three children in 10 years and out went my plans for continuing law school. At that time in the 60s, early 70s, universities and professional schools outside of NYC were not very encouraging to night students, especially women. Before we'd met, I'd been in a night law school, as only one of four women in the entire school. Now as I sought to reenter, the schools considered me unacceptable. As a homemaker in my mid-30s, and female, the prevailing advice was "don't waste our time." "Study counseling," they advised. So, I had our third child and instead took a masters' degree in history, at night, in an area about which I'd never taken a single course in undergrad school. And my husband, the avocational historian, encouraged me all the way, expecting that I would, like him, top off my education with a doctorate. I preferred reentering the business world and testing out my creativity.

Years later, as our dual careers tossed in the recessionary winds of the '80s, Herb and I decided to merge talents and differing expertise into business together. My great fear was that my husband and partner would discover I was really not as smart as he thought I was. In truth, I was also afraid he would dominate. I didn't mind having him carry the title of president so long as both of us were equal in responsibility and recognition. We merged my area of strategic communications with his knowledge base of high tech and Silicon Valley, and our company actually became very successful. A west coast client even boasted to his Hong Kong bankers about his Shaker Heights' boutique High Tech PR firm. As long as my husband could explain the specific technology, its innovations and benefits for users, I could then strategically position and communicate this message to their users, media and the world.

We even shared writing. I wove together cotton candy, media placement, and basic thrust. Through sneaker software I would write the first draft and he would apply his strategic management, discipline, and technical expertise to the second draft. It then came back to me to massage and produce draft three. The combo was a winner and through our guidance numerous startup companies found their limelight and grew.

Neither of us sought empire. We just wanted to do the best work we could for our clients and to do it the most comfortably for ourselves. We worked out of our home and made the paneled basement into our fully equipped office with desks positioned only three feet from each other. Our basic personalities sometimes clashed. I needed absolute silence when creating a new article, speech or positioning statement. He preferred the radio. Loud. From his think-tank and consulting days, Herb expected clients to follow his advice almost like from the Sermon on the Mount. From my agency days, I was the more pragmatic and knew convincing sometimes meant doing things both ways: theirs and the right way so clients could make a more informed choice.

Probably our biggest challenges came over disagreements about our kids. Both of us had experienced difficult childhoods. Herb followed the controlling grooves and conditioning from his. And I rejected mine and sought more latitude for them. I especially disagreed with "the father knows best" attitudes of this period and wanted our children, much like our clients, to experience freedom to make guided choices. Those were not easy days for us, or our kids. In fact, it was the most turbulent period of our marriage, with frequent clashes, and not one I'd care to revisit.

But now as I look down at my husband lightly sleeping in his hospital bed, the comforter up under his chin, I think about these nineteen post-stroke years, and how we somehow made this almost one-third of our marriage work. Even bracketed by a wheelchair, and a medical suitcase, we traveled, sometimes by plane, often by car. We saw plays, attended lectures, loved restaurants, appreciated being with friends. The point was to enjoy quality time, a reason for both of us to keep going. Our fifteen years in business together provided us sufficient funds for trips, twice to Turks & Caicos and three times to Cancun, as we continued to search out destinations that offered us accessibility.

There were unusual challenges, including figuring out how to change a wet Depends on a long, United Airlines flight, but the support of others allowed us the dignity of dependence. We mastered these and a host of other challenges as well. More than anything else, I learned to love and value this special person who was himself facing a changing dynamic that I could barely imagine. And now, at this phase, I've even learned to climb over the rails of his hospital bed and lay next to him so that he knows he is not alone. I deeply remember the husband I've lost over time and love the husband I'm trying so hard to protect now. Love is flexible and as stretchable as one requires.

Am I ready in this period of home hospice to let my husband, the love of my life, go? This question keeps me up most nights as I ponder when and how to let go. Obviously, I want him to go gently into the good night, in comfort and pain free. When do I stop fighting and let the next infection take over? I'm close but I'm not there yet. It will be soon. And then I'll have to say goodbye.

When Comfort and Care Aren't So Comforting

Herb's decline continued and, by the beginning of November, 2019, I also brought in a hospice team associated with the skilled nursing facility we'd used previously. That was not a good decision.

Herb and I already had all the 24/7[4] team, equipment, designated bedroom and Medicare-provided hospital bed. We'd ordered the bed through our internist the previous June, recognizing our need to be prepared for the final phase. With these big pieces of the puzzle already in place, this hospice wanted more.

Even the name of the hospice group "Comfort & Care" was deceptive. From the beginning, this hospice insisted that we change our hospital bed so their organization could bill Medicare directly. I questioned why we needed to remove one bed and install another when Herb was already bedridden. The hospice nurse, Kathy, assured me

---

4   24 hours a day, 7 days a week

that she would take care of everything and be there with us to oversee a smooth exchange. She cancelled at the last minute. All hell broke out late that Friday afternoon when two trucks and delivery services stood outside, waiting at the same time. After the first bed was removed, I saw that the second delivery man carried in the replacement without railings.

This situation was wholly unacceptable. Herb was at a squirmy stage and had already fallen out of bed multiple times. I informed the men from both companies that they would have to remain through the entire night, and perhaps the entire weekend, each guarding one side of the new hospital bed. The first company, which had already removed all their equipment, volunteered to retrieve and leave the bed rails. Later, with the bed and Herb both reinstalled, the two men heaved sighs of relief and went home. The delinquent nurse later called apologizing and admitted that she had neglected to order the railings. She offered to come the next day, Saturday, and bring other medical supplies she should have brought with her on that cancelled Friday. I declined. She insisted.

The following afternoon, a Saturday, instead of seeing Kathy I received a phone reprimand from the hospice director, Judy, sternly informing me that her staff required their weekends off. She obviously didn't know Herb's history of squirming off the bed and lambasted me for insisting on the railings, saying that the state of Ohio no longer required these. This was not a good way to begin a relationship designed to bring me "comfort and care."

As months moved on and Herb's death became closer, that same hospice nurse insistently pushed me about my plans after Herb passed as though it were her ordained mission to have an answer. From the beginning, people had continually queried me about what I was going to do after he died. Early on I usually responded with a droll comment because I hated this question: "I'll find a gigolo." When that response grew stale, I claimed assuredly that I'd jump on a freighter and travel to ports Herb and I had never visited before. Then, when I finally I took time to investigate the freighter website I discovered these working ships have a stated policy not to accept passengers aged 80 and over.

Unhappily, that excluded me although I certainly would be more than willing to take a stress test to prove my capabilities and stamina.

This time, I flippantly responded, "Well, maybe I'll just take some pills," my retort because I neither liked this nurse nor her questioning.

This was not the expected response. Although the nurse had no way of knowing that I was obviously joking, or that I have a life threatening-adverse reaction to all meds, including aspirin. Her eyes bulged when she heard my response. Alarms went off. She immediately reported me for being suicidal, without follow up or opportunity for defense, to authorities. The medical director of the hospice appeared at my home the next evening, a dark, stormy Saturday night in the middle of winter, without prior notice, to check me out. I now had to prove my sanity to this physician and inform him why my remark was jocular and made no sense. This nurse's kneejerk reaction taught me never again to wisecrack, especially about my end-of-life plans. I now wondered whether Herb would be removed from our home and put into foster care.

The following Monday morning, I sat the nurse down at our dining room table. My intention was to review what had happened over the weekend and expressly remind her about the Hypocritic oath "to do no harm" that medical professionals are supposed to follow. She ran out of my home without seeing Herb for his regularly scheduled appointment and we never intersected again.

The replacement nurse, Meredith, was thoughtful, kind, and non-intrusive. And I made no further joking comments. While I liked her very much, I had continuing problems with the hospice, including their rationing of bed pads and wipes and a mutual sense of mistrust. I chose not to change hospices, even knowing I could, because I did not want to have a third go-around with still another hospital bed. But this relationship added greatly to my stress and I wound up in the emergency room of the Cleveland Clinic on two consecutive days that November because of stress and extremely high blood pressure.

Preparing Family and Friends

Most of our family and friends assumed that our limbo state could go on forever. Toward the end of 2019, I reached out to prepare them (and myself) that Herb had begun hospice, the final stage.

To Family and Friends,

After a long battle against stroke and other chronic issues, Herb has earned the right to comfort and rest. It breaks my heart but I also recognize that, from love, this is the time to let him go gently into the good night.

On meeting Herb in Baltimore for the first time, I fell in love with:

- The boy from Brooklyn who also read the NEW YORK TIMES daily…
- Who had a strong yearning to use academics to open his world
- Whose MBA advisor at NYU was the management guru Peter Drucker
- Who believed in the early 60s that the integrated circuit would open the world
- Who the mid 1960s predicted in his doctoral dissertation that it would bring about a revolution in technology opening to personal as well as quantum computers, cell phones, robotics, AI and so much more
- Who earned his doctorate in management and economics from George Washington University in 3 years. At night.
- Who counseled that Cleveland could join in this magic moment if only it would cut away from the old, staid manufacturing mindset
- Who conveyed his urging through annual columns in Crain's "CLEVELAND BUSINESS" (even after his massive stroke in 2001).

I will miss my best friend, lover, partner, and husband who struggled so hard to live and hung around long enough to help me see my way to old age. My world will never be the same.

Herb did pass early the following April, at home as I'd promised him, but not comfortably at the end. He could barely move or eat and he had few words. Often now I climbed over the bars into his hospice bed and held him. Tears ran down his eyes as I recounted trips and periods in our lives together that we'd enjoyed. Herb's last words to me before he went silent in the last couple of days was that he loved me. I knew how uncomfortable he was. Even though I had the key to the hospice lock box with morphine, I stayed within the assigned but very limited dosage. I regret not taking the initiative and doubling it to make him more comfortable. But I knew I was already viewed as an "difficult woman" and that I was being watched closely.

Wondering how other couples dealt with end-of-life care, I interviewed Sheila, a friend over many years. "Michael was sick for a year but we didn't anticipate his dying. Taking a lesson from you, I stayed with him 24/7 in the hospital and at home," Sheila explains. In realizing he was at the end, "We were both able to cope because we'd had a good life. And knowing he was content with his life was helpful."

For others who are quoted later, death more often came suddenly with little warning. I obviously had the longest lead time for planning.

Lessons Learned

1. *Treasure every day as a gift.* Remember to verbally share your love and affection because the time and void will come.
2. *Bring on caregivers who are warm and supportive.* Not all of them are. Many move functionally from one job to another and use the nighttime shift for their own sleep. I often woke to Herb's cries and responded first.
3. *Choose a hospice based on recommendation* from more than one person. Meet the nurses and physician who will be on your team. Change if displeased.
4. *Make end-of-life decisions while your loved one is clear-minded* and can voice his/her own needs and expectations. This includes not only choice of burial plot or cremation but also the service and eulogies, as preferred.[5]
5. *Update medical power of attorney and resuscitation requirements.* Weigh your decisions carefully and together, if

---

5   End-of-life decisions should be made long before the death bed scenario. There should be no surprises.

possible. With Covid-19 treatment, and end-of-life hospital care, we are now finding that ventilators are not always the key to returning good health and this death can be very agonizingly painful.

6. ***Consider options--whether to die in a nursing home or at home.*** Sometimes nursing- home care can be more expensive than home care, which is tabulated by the hour, day and night. And nursing home care under these Covid-conditions can be isolating.

7. ***Know that you can fire a hospice*** should you find the service and support not to your liking.

8. ***Insist upon meeting the physician and director in charge of the hospice*** because you may have questions and you need to know exactly which services they offer. Communication is not always direct and some hospices use physicians only as "consultants" allowing minimal, if any, direct contact.

9. ***Home hospices provide bathing and grooming.*** Be sure an aide conveys dignity and respect during this most vulnerable time.

10. ***Visit the chapel or funeral home in advance,*** when you can, even if just to check out available services and cost. Don't allow surprises to bombard you at the last minute.[6]

---

6   This assumes that you have advance notice of impending death. Obviously not all of us have that warning. But for most seniors, even those without illness, advance thought and preparation will save future stress and confusion later.

CHAPTER III

MOURNING DURING A PANDEMIC

Herb turned to me any number of times, especially as he became weaker and less able to transfer out of the bed, "Why does this take so long?" He was uncomfortable, miserable, and often cried from frustration as he sequentially lost control of his basic body functions. He begged me to do something to move the process along. Much as I believe in compassionate death, I eyed that special hospice-designated lock box with fear. Everything had to be recorded and I'd learned previously from this hospice not to joke, exaggerate or break any rules.

Final Steps

We were no longer affiliated with a congregation or temple. Our children were grown and we had drawn away during Herb's post-stroke decades when it became so hard to park and move about. In late November 2019, I contacted a rabbi and neighbor whom I'd met informally at several of our street block-parties over recent years. I asked for his help in scoping out Herb's funeral since I had no idea how to plan this, was not a current member, and needed to be prepared. Rabbi Steven Segar came to our home and we talked at the dining room table. I confided my thoughts about both a non-traditional funeral service and cremation and asked whether he would officiate in a Hebrew service under these circumstances.[7]

I'd already spoken with the Berkowitz-Kumin-Bookatz Memorial Chapel about the service; engaged a young flutist from the Cleveland Institute of Music to play two pieces I thought Herb would like, and arranged for two actor friends to read from a William Shakespeare

---

7   Cremation is not readily accepted in both conservative and orthodox spectrums of Judaism although the concept is slowly gaining greater acceptance in the former.

sonnet and an E.E. Cummings poem I loved. In addition, I hoped to include several eulogies along with traditional prayers. Rabbi Segar approved and later he even went upstairs to meet and say a prayer for the dying over Herb. Little did I expect Herb to make it into the new year but he did.

This freedom to choose and define a burial service seems to vary in different religious observances. A Catholic friend recalled that in three consecutive burials for his parents and brother he had little choice or input other than to fill out a standard questionnaire provided by the church. There was much that was ceremonial but little directly personal and eulogies were excluded.

Herb made it into the Covid-19 pandemic as well. He died on April 3, a Friday morning at 3 a.m. His wonderful "24/7" ladies, Shondra and Pique, lovingly washed and prepared him. The hospice nurse arrived to confirm his death; and within the hour he was transported to the funeral home.

Announcement to Family and Friends

Dear Family and Friends,

It is with great sadness that I must share news that Herb passed away at home today, April 3, at 3 a.m. after a 20-year epic battle. Because of Covid-19 precautions there will be no formal memorial to bid him off. Instead, we will have a very small, backyard service this Sunday (subject to Ohio regulations and crowd limitations.) A webcast of this service will be announced later. Obviously, there will be no Shiva or personal visitations. For anyone wishing to make a contribution to honor Herb's memory, please consider The Cooper Union for the Advancement of Science and Art[8], http://www.cooper.edu/. Or to a preferred charity of your choice. There are so many in need now. Please stay well.

Berenice and Family

---

8   Herb's Alma Mata.

The Memorial Service

The coronavirus obviously changed our well-formed plans. The chapel was now closed. The service took place in our own backyard four days later, on a cold, raw Palm Sunday, April 5, at 11 a.m. We were limited by government mandate to just 10 people, masked and spaced well apart. A few neighbors also stood in our driveway so as not to raise our count. The funeral home had set up chairs. Steve designed and arranged a variety of high-tech speakers, computers and video equipment so that along with my comments the service would also transfer and record eulogies from both my daughter, Kathy, with her family, in Falls Church, Virginia, and Herb's 90-year-old brother Bill, in Atlanta, Georgia. Rabbi Segar and I wore masks and we spoke into a mic amplified by Steve's sound system.

The weather was raw and miserable but the service, which lasted about one-half hour, was warm and loving, and was followed by friends who shared their own remembrances. Overnight, Steve and his friends from around the U.S. worked online to splice and assemble a beautiful video incorporating the entire service that we shared with family and friends around the world.

I've found over the years attending funeral services of many different faiths that it is unusual for the surviving spouse to deliver a eulogy, although there is no injunction either way. I felt no one else could say what I had to share and stepped forward because I owed it to my husband and, yes, even myself, to do so. As with everything else, I'd prepared this in advance and had read it to Herb who listened carefully and included an additional point that was very important to him. In highlighting his accomplishments, he wanted me to say that he'd earned his doctorate in three years, at night, and working full time, a distinction he was obviously so proud of.

Our service was personal, warm, even intimate. I think Herb would have appreciated, maybe even enjoyed, the comments, style and informality and especially the high tech that Steve incorporated.

Kathy and her partner Mark Massey arranged the "Shiva" commemoration the following day on Zoom. It included family and friends located around the world. According to Jewish tradition Shiva follows burial and usually stretches over seven days, excluding Shabbat, where family and friends come to pay their respects. I've often thought of this as similar to a concentrated wake that Christian friends have before the burial.

Also, in my tradition, there are prayers morning and evening for a full month. The spouse follows this observance for 30 days. In contrast, our online Shiva lasted only about two hours. The rest of the mourning was up to me alone, supported by Steve and limited by sequestering, quarantining and masks. No hugs. Few potlucks. Even fewer visitations and phone calls. And there were certainly no bereavement groups to follow.

While Herb's loss came as no surprise, I found it especially difficult to go from full motion as a wife, caregiver and activist to a state of being utterly rudderless. This global pandemic not only exacerbated my personal emptiness but has taken away the lives of millions of people of all ages, their lives, jobs and security.

My Eulogy for Herb, 4/5/20

Herb stayed as long as he could. I truly believe he did that for me because he knew how afraid I was to have him leave me. Some people said we were joined at the hip. Others said it was the brain. But I always knew we were joined at the heart.

Many friends and family members who knew us well were afraid for our impending marriage and worried that with our competitive personalities we would kill one another within the first two weeks. Well, we made it through 56 ½ years, 3 children, and a terrific business partnership.

Herb was a hard-headed man, stubborn and no great fan of fluids. But he was a good man, a loving husband and my best friend. He was also a man with a keen intellect, a desire to see Cleveland grow in high tech similar to the Silicon Valley scene he'd studied so closely both for his doctoral dissertation and subsequent career in monitoring the high-tech field. He loved theater, music, art (even though it took some urging to nudge him forward from Andrew Wyeth's "Christina's World" to Miro). He admitted he wasn't a great father/grandfather. It was hard for him to step away from the conditional upbringing he himself found so familiar. He did try to do better as our three children (Kathy, Miriam, and Steve) and four grandchildren (Sam, Robin, Zack and Max) grew to adulthood. And he recognized and regretted his failures.

And one more thing. When we were saying our goodbyes, I asked if there was anything additional he wanted me to share. He took a breath and said to say that he'd done his doctorate in under 3 years. At night. And in person.

I'd hoped we could stretch our time even longer. But after 19+ years post-stroke, Herb knew it was time to let go. Life and breath became too hard to sustain and it wasn't fair to keep him to his promise.

I will miss my husband, friend, partner, and the love of my life. This will be a difficult journey forward.

So, goodnight sweet prince. May flights of angels sing thee to thy rest.

Herb's Obituary

Herb Kleiman passed away on April 3, 2020 at his home in Shaker Heights after an epic 20-year battle against massive stroke.

He served as president of Kleiman Associates Inc., a strategic marketing-communications firm serving high technology companies nationwide that he and his wife Berenice formed as equal partners in 1987. He and Berenice co-authored "ONE STROKE, TWO SURVIVORS" one of their two books published by the Cleveland Clinic that recounted their battle against his stroke in 2001. The book is written in two voices, that of the stroke survivor and the spousal caregiver. For four decades before forming Kleiman Associates, Herb worked with top managements as a high-tech management consultant, Wall Street high-tech securities analyst, and then as a business leader and strategist. His numerous articles, op-ed columns and speeches helped translate and position complex and often fast-changing technologies. As a member of the Cleveland Engineering Society, he founded and chaired its Management of Technology Division.

Herb held business degrees from George Washington University (DBA) and New York University (MBA). He earned his first degree in electrical engineering (BSEE) from The Cooper Union. His 1966 doctoral dissertation about the birth of the microchip remains a seminal contribution to the history of 20th century technology. He gifted The Stanford University Library with the collection of his oral history interviews with key pioneers in microelectronics conducted for his doctoral dissertation.

Herb is survived by his wife of 56 years Berenice (nee Elkin), his children Kathy Kleiman (Mark Massey), Miriam Kleiman (Jason Steinbaum) and Steven Kleiman; grandchildren Jonathan and Robin Stern, and Zachary and Maxwell Steinbaum A memorial service may be held at some time in the future. There will be no Shiva. Contributions may be made to The Cooper Union, 30 Cooper Sq, New York, NY 10003.

Photo Credit to Norman Becker

Herb's beautiful urn sits on our dining room buffet and I pat his lid every morning. Knowing that he's here with me brings comfort. Steve has the instruction that, when I die, he is to mingle both our ashes and distribute them in a lake, river, or ocean so that we flow off together.

Other Experiences

It's been pointed out to me that my experiences with Herb's dying and death were relatively straightforward, and not really typical. But I also brought to this long-held negative feelings about the burial service and any overlap with food. My mother died only weeks after I'd graduated from college. In our small village in upstate New York, no one sent trays nor did my father and older brothers have any guidance about ordering platters. We were all stupefied by the suddenness of her passing, especially since my kid-sister was only ten years old.

So, at 21, I found myself in the kitchen cooking hardboiled eggs, opening cans, and mixing tuna and mayonnaise for egg and tuna salads to feed guests who sat in the living room after the service expecting to be served lunch. I'm sure the food was extra salty from my tears that fell into the mixing. From that point on I have never taken more than coffee at a Shiva visit and I still recoil with embedded resentment.

Steve understood my aversion toward serving food and assumed the responsibility for going out early in the morning and buying bagels, cream cheese, drinks, and then setting up tables in our freezing back yard with all the utensils. Friends and neighbors also brought baked goods and I prepared a huge pot of coffee.

Again, without sustaining membership in a religious congregation Steve and I were adrift, not unlike many people today who are also unaffiliated. I am well aware that others who are better connected often benefit from communal support. I've witnessed how synagogue committees organize and provide their member families with dinner trays each night for the length of their Shiva. Often one person is designated to coordinate the community efforts. A rabbi, accompanied by members of the congregation, friends and family comes to the home to lead the Shiva memorial services each evening. Even had we had that support, which we didn't, during this pandemic it would have been impossible. Restaurants were closed and people were not traveling or mingling. Steve and I were isolated and alone.

Curious about this death and dying sequence, I set out to see how other spouses have fared in their mourning cycle even without Covid-19. I found a broad range of experiences, from the middle of the night call from the hospital to sudden death on a cruise.

Many of us have bought into the myth that most people die gently in bed, often in their sleep. Of the more than 40 people whom I've interviewed for this book I haven't encountered even one spouse who did. As a matter of fact, few reported a gentle death under any circumstances.

Manjula

Manjula's husband, a cardiac specialist, diagnosed his own heart problem but received little support from the hospital treating him, world renown for cardiac care. Plied with fluids, he was discharged with a 50-pound overnight weight gain that was suffocating him. He died at home within 24 hours. His hospice care had only begun the previous day. The hospice did, however, direct Manju to a funeral home that offered cremation service and hosted a small family gathering to say goodbye. Even though Manju too is a physician and psychiatrist, she was surprised at the suddenness of her husband's death. "I am a denier." Still the paperwork was basically in place and everything else was straight forward. The funeral home ordered the death certificates and, with their intact joint wills, few last-minute decisions needed to be made.

Rena

Rena, on the other hand was totally caught by surprise. As snowbirds spending the winter in Tampa, she and husband Howard were in the midst of deciding which restaurant to go to for dinner that evening when he suddenly suffered a massive stroke in mid-sentence. Howard never regained consciousness and succumbed in a Florida hospital four days later.

Arriving back at home in New Jersey only three days before Christmas, she found their New Jersey rabbi and cantor both away on vacation. Since the assistant rabbi and Howard had not been on the best of terms, Rena moved the funeral service to her daughter's synagogue, also in New Jersey. There, as an outsider she received little advice or direction from either rabbi or funeral home, selected at the last minute to accommodate family logistics within the greater New York/New Jersey sprawl.

Rena and Howard had arranged their cemetery plots years earlier but everything else she remembers became jumbled. Howard, an attorney, had covered most of the legal aspects and had everything in order. But even that advance did not go smoothly and created a series of family problems. A large luncheon arranged by a family member resulted in an unexpectedly large bill sent directly to Rena. Her brother, also an attorney and designated by Howard as executor to the estate, chose to avoid issues in the will contested by one of her children. He cancelled shortly afterward and left Rena adrift and alone to find legal and accounting support.

Rae

Rae was on a Royal Caribbean cruise with her husband and returning to Baltimore, their home base. They were one stop short of their return destination when Manny suddenly died. Had his death come earlier in their cruise she would have been forced to disembark elsewhere. Rae found the ship's captain and crew "wonderfully accommodating." He even provided a land line without charge so she could contact her rabbi and children. She was permitted to be among the first to disembark and meet her waiting son. Meanwhile, her rabbi had contacted the funeral home to coordinate removal of the body and plan the service. Looking back, Rae says "Manny had loved cruising and he died doing what he liked to do." On disembarking, she still clutched the special photograph of the happy couple taken at dinner the previous evening.

Rae found few subsequent surprises but she remembers lots of paperwork that followed. "It took time to take care of everything but Manny and I had had that conversation and I knew what had to be done." Rae adds, "I think the fact that I had worked before marriage was a plus because I knew how to manage my checking account and funds." She even found a cooperative Social Security administrator who allowed her to establish her husband's death with just a basic form from the funeral chapel.

Bob

Bob's wife Linda died alone in a nursing home during the Covid-19 virus. That home was closed to all visitors, family included. She had been in the home for several years. Because of her combination of both Parkinson's and dementia he was no longer able to care for her at home, even with 24/7 support. Bob and his children tried to communicate by Facetime but she was too weak to even hear their goodbyes. At her few moments of clarity, Linda said she wanted her torture to be over. Her funeral service was limited to very few in attendance, following state rules, and broader Zoom for outlying friends and family. The severity of this isolation and subsequent mourning will continue to haunt Bob and his family.

Lessons Learned

1. *Be prepared.* None of us will live forever. Both you and your spouse should agree and plan together for your deaths. And there should be no surprises, especially at this time of such great loss and sadness.
2. *Make your plans readily available and accessible to others* in case of mutual demise.
3. *Also prepare your eulogy and obituary* in advance. Don't think of this as being macabre because, considering the options, there isn't much opportunity or time to think under pressure.
4. *Confirm that your chapel or funeral service will distribute the news release to appropriate newspapers* and list any on-line announcements. There is usually a minor charge.
5. *Select a photo of the deceased to accompany this obituary.*
6. *For those who are computer savvy consider your own email announcement* to friends and family.
7. *Refer to your selected funeral chapel as your guide.* They are knowledgeable and experienced in the basic steps required to report the death, will order the death certificates, and even provide chairs for Shiva, a home service. This is all included in their fees.
8. *Should you choose cremation,* as we did, make sure the service is an accredited facility and affiliated with your religion.
9. *Consider plans for out of town guests* who wish to be part of your family service.

10. Delegate responsibilities to other family members--when you can to organize food following the service. Although some may send trays or pastries, or organize dinners, that is not always the case. Be prepared.

CHAPTER IV

SURVIVING LOSS

Death and dying for many families usually present a time for families to be together and share strength, support and fond memories. But it's been hard to mourn and grieve during a pandemic surrounded by panic and fear of contagion. With no visitors because cities, planes, and movement were locked down, my world came to a standstill.

Quarantining for Steve and me had already begun in early April when Herb died. People who might ordinarily have joined us, including our out-of-town family and friends, hung back behind their own closed doors afraid to travel or breach state and county orders.

Son Steve, undeterred by quarantines, came home from Florida as soon as I called to tell him that Herb was in his last days. He drove day and night and arrived within two days. Other family members, unable to travel under these circumstances, mourned at home. Steve and I were alone except for a few intrepid friends and several thoughtful neighbors. Passover, which began three days following our service, passed over without attention. There was no point in observing. We and the friends whom we traditionally invited to share our Seders certainly weren't in the mood for festivities. The world we previously knew was hidden behind loss, masks and fear.

Respite

Steve recognized something that I didn't. Since Herb and I had been travelers I required some modicum of "normalcy" to break away from this solitariness for my own mental balance. Over the next three consecutive Sundays he planned drives for us far away from Cleveland. On the first Sunday, only one week following Herb's memorial service, we drove to Detroit, Michigan, ostensibly to visit the Packard manufacturing ruins. It was a three and a half-hour drive each way. Steve loaded his phone with podcasts that he knew I would like.

The drive was companionable. We stopped for MacDonald's and other fast food take-outs along the way and back. Steve, in a more advanced stage of high tech than I, amazed me by driving through the through lanes to collect our order just by flashing his iPhone. No other payment or touch was necessary.

Once in front of the crumbling Packard plant, he encouraged me to climb with him over the fence to explore the inside ruins. I demurred saying that I hadn't had a recent tetanus shot. Later we toured suburban and downtown areas where the tale of two cities was obvious. I called the entire scenario "the planet of the apes" because of the vast crumbling wreckage, including the downtown center where high rise office buildings with broken windows stood against new development and even a monorail. The highlight was La Belle Isle, a magnificent park located in the Detroit River between Detroit and Winsor, Ontario. On that sunny, spring afternoon, it was a pleasure to see many people meandering through the park, only a few wearing face-masks. The visitor center and gas station bathrooms remained closed. Fortunately, we later found a Whelan's Drug Store with men's and women's bathrooms open and available.

More Travels with Steve

The following Sunday we drove south three hours to Columbus, where we'd lived for eleven years, and visited good friends while standing six feet apart. In preparation for the trip Steve had emailed me a list of possible sites to review and I chose three sites: a Confederate cemetery I'd never known about, a topiary park in the center of the downtown, and Battelle Memorial Institute on the west side, near Ohio State University, where Herb had worked. On our return trip we stopped in Marion, Ohio and visited the tombs of Warren and Florence Harding.

The third Sunday was my responsibility although I neglected to do the detailed research that Steve expected of me, especially to identify places that specifically were open during this pandemic. I chose Buffalo and came up with a couple of parks and the Forest Lawn Cemetery.[9]

9   Forest Lawn Cemetery, a historic cemetery in Buffalo, New York, was founded in 1849 and has a number of distinguished people buried there, including U.S. President Millard Fillmore, First Lady Abigail Fillmore, along with a special memorial designed by Frank Lloyd Wright for a dear friend.

Steve extended my proposed meanderings by adding the Niagara Falls Park (American side), which unlike most of the places on my original list was also unlocked.

Again, our biggest challenge was finding a bathroom. With visitor centers and most bathrooms closed it took an anxious shuffle until we found open doors. The remaining walk around the falls was relaxed and wonderful. The sun was shining and we joined lots of people of all ages, some wearing masks, others escorting their dogs on leashes, and most maintaining a satisfactory distance.

Steve Was Right.

These drives were energizing, lifted my dour mood, and helped restore a balance to loss that sequestering at home alone would only deepen. He left on the fourth Sunday and I was on my own. I drove by myself to the Mentor Headlands, a beach at the northernmost point of Ohio, on the shore of Lake Erie. There I sat on a log watching swimmers and families, even a couple of boats, and just depressurizing. I hadn't realized how deeply tired I was. Just sitting and watching helped me recoup a little. I'd brought no books, had no plans, and was alone without even a blanket.

Sitting there I felt no guilt, only the huge chasm of loss. Since 2001, I had focused my efforts on Herb, doing my best to love and care for him and now was absolutely rudderless. While he was in the rehab hospital, I'd closed our consulting business and reworked our lives to make recovery easier and better for him. Now watching the bathers, especially families with young children, I found myself thinking and pondering the difference between loneliness and being alone. I desperately missed my husband, missed being a wife, and, even more, missed being Herb's wife.

Over these years I'd adjusted to each decline in his condition. Even when he no longer could do much to help me, or himself, I felt secure knowing we were still together. Now I was truly alone with no one to talk to at night or share my day trips. No one to share dinner with. No one to read the NY TIMES' editorials and op-eds to. What now?

Spousal Breakdown and Survival

Physical deterioration by the surviving spouse is a phenomenon now gaining greater recognition these days. As part of my research, I've since talked with other widows and widowers who, even in pre-pandemic times, experienced their own health declines shortly after bereavement, including a variety of life-threatening illnesses, from Crohn's disease, stroke and shingles and accidents to the very current Covid-19.

I myself had two unusual falls in the first four months following Herb's passing, a huge surprise because my balance is really good, am generally resilient, and I exercise daily. Both falls were directly onto my face with the suddenness that didn't allow for any intermediate bracing. I am now seeing a retinal specialist for what threatens to become a retinal tear. A close medical friend of mine speculates that after almost 20 years as a caregiver actively monitoring everything around me, I simply shut off and wasn't paying attention. While these events might be considered coincidence, evidence is accumulating anecdotally that this type of reaction and subsequent threats to the surviving spouse are more widespread than previously assumed.

Talking with Joyce I've learned that in the first few years since her husband Saul's passing she's endured a continuing series of maladies, from shingles to broken wrists, to hip replacement, and more recently Covid-19. My sister-in-law Lois suffered a massive stroke within the first month after my brother's passing and later, within a year, the amputation of her right leg.

Margaret began dealing with Lyme disease, Crohn's, and a series of other auto immune and digestive issues only months after John died. Another friend, Sheila, underwent sequential knee-replacement surgeries almost immediately following Michael's passing. How many of these medical issues directly relate to the physical and mental stresses after loss can't be directly proven. But they do raise an open question: whether spousal caregivers, because they often ignore or postpone their own medical problems as widows and widowers, are finally forced to pay attention to an accumulating avalanche of their own needs? Or is there more? Perhaps reaction to the full dynamic of the loss itself?

Recent medical research at the Cleveland Clinic has introduced the phenomenon of "broken heart syndrome" now recognized as one of the most stressful disorders that can threaten the survivor. This situation is underscored when elderly couples, backed by decades-long relationships, die within days of each other. More immediately, Covid-19's human-interest stories have drawn much coverage by television news during the last year, particularly when older couples, lying in adjacent hospital beds, die within hours of each other.

Jane Brody, in a Sept. 28, 2016 NYTimes' column about widowhood, described three factors that influence overall resilience:[10]

1) *Reliable comfort--having someone to confide in or lean on in times of trouble, and being able to get help from other people when needed;*

2) *Social connectedness—whether their physical health or emotional problems interfered with social activities like visiting friends and interacting socially with neighbors or groups, and*

3) *Daily functioning—overcoming difficulties with their normal activities because of emotional problems like depression or anxiety.*

Combine bereavement with a pandemic, eliminating the support above, and the stakes become even higher.

Where Are Our Friends?

Death is lonely and loss of a mate is when you most need your friends for social connectedness. But the reaction and sudden mysterious disappearance of these friends is certainly echoed by my own experience and by the many widows and widowers whom I've recently interviewed—pandemic or not. We've all experienced the "friends" who pay the token call, send a token gift, and then disappear. Either they consider bereavement as contagious or find your situation too troublesome and inconvenient remains for them to answer. Most won't. Joyce, in our interview, described how, over a 40-year span, parents of a close friend played bridge once a week and vacationed every year

10   NEW YORK TIMES TUESDAY SCIENCE SECTION, "Widowhood: the belief that over 60% of bereaved people resiliently bounce back, not so."

with their best friends, a couple who lived across the street. When her friend's father died, that ended the bridge and trips. The wife of the remaining couple continued to have lunch with her friend's mother once in a while, never with the husband included, and even that tapered off pretty quickly as well. Sadly, there are many comparable stories.

It upset me that some of my/our friends of long duration also followed this pattern. I was particularly irked by M. from our single days whom I considered as my special friend as well as Herb's college buddy. True, he wasn't that great after Herb's stroke either but this absence crossed a red line for me. I sent him an email letter expressing my disappointment. His response that came almost immediately was that "This wasn't what he did." I can only assume he referred to showing compassion although he stated that "he felt Herb's loss in his heart." I've since erased his name from my contact list with the satisfaction that at least I'd expressed my thoughts. My brother-in-law, serving as an intermediary (his choice), reported how unhappy my comment had made this absent ex-friend feel.

Deafening silence like this adds to my own loneliness and isolation. Invisibility hurts deeply. I don't expect people to prostrate themselves with condolences but a call once in a while shouldn't be so awful. Over the years Herb and I reached out to many people, professionally and otherwise, through good times and bad, and often included single, married, gay, divorced and widowed friends in our dinner gatherings. Other of my widowed friends share much the same reaction as mine. Widows report that over the decades, while they were the ones who maintained the planning and socializing, these ties ended abruptly with their husband's deaths. Widowers also echo similar feelings about abandonment. Speculation may be that this change of status can "threaten" a "friend's" marriage. That doesn't make much sense to me but what's the point of arguing? I've already tried that and struck out.

The really bright spots, now special favorites, are often shared by friends and neighbors with whom we had only limited ties previously and who have stepped forward with open arms, notes, and memorial contributions in Herb's name. I cherish the calls and notes I continue to receive from so many past and current friends and their children.

Emails and Letters from Friends

My dear friend. Herb's long nightmare is over and now he is in the light. I weep with you while knowing and understanding your depth of weariness, I know your depth of sorrow is even greater. I am with you in all my thoughts. You have truly been a north star. I hope you can rest some now my friend. If there is anything I can do to help you, please ask. Feel the embrace of condolences and love I send to you. –Margaret

Dear Berenice,
Thank you for sending the written copy of your eulogy. This did help me understand much more how Herb and you loved each other and how tight your partnership has been. Even if I heard the sound of video, I would have so many difficulties in understanding what was spoken in the video. (Maybe less than 10%. As I get old my English-hearing capability has tremendously declined.) I directly interpreted our Japanese idiomatic expression into English. In these three months, most of TV programs are filled by news of coronavirus spread and many parts of these are about the serious situation in New York. I think Shaker Heights area is safe, but please take care for this problem. Fondly, –Hiroshi (Tokyo)

Hi Aunt Berenice,
I'm so sorry to hear this news. I know that it has been a very difficult journey for you, but you were such an exceptional partner and caretaker for Uncle Herb. I'm sorry that we will not be able to visit for the funeral or Shiva, but please know that we are thinking of you and sending lots of love in your direction. – Jeff (Baltimore)

Dear Berenice,
Tough times made harder. There would have been no epic battle for Herbert without you - the soldier,

platoon leader, corporal lieutenant and General. Truly two survivors --for a long, long time. I wish each of my patients had an advocate like you to help them navigate healthcare. My thoughts are with you. –Anne (Houston)

Berenice,
Herb battled on remarkably for such a long time, aided by your love and support. He was a man of great character and intelligence, though not always easy to live with as so many people of that caliber are. I was pleased to call him a friend over all that time since 1969 when you generously put up a couple of impoverished students [from England] in your home in Columbus. Quite unwittingly, he and I were researching what became the lynchpin of our modern electronic world though he could see that more clearly than me. Let's keep in touch.
–Tony and Gill (London)

Berenice,
In your trials over the past years, you and Herb have touched other lives without, perhaps, even knowing it. The love and devotion the two of you have demonstrated in your personal lives has not gone unnoticed. I can honestly say that you two are an example of what the real thing is all about. It's a lot more than cards, flowers and candy on Valentine's Day. There will be tough days and tough times. We've watched the two of you take them on, caring for and loving each other all the way. Thanks for the lessons about what real love means. God bless both of you. –Ed (Cleveland)

I responded to each letter, card and gift with handwritten notes to thank our friends around the world for their thoughtfulness. My only frustration was that my appreciation was tardy because most recipient organizations took several months to send the names of those gifting.

Lessons Learned

1. ***Consider seeking professional bereavement support*** from a grief counselor, social worker or psychologist.

2. ***Communicate with others during this period of enforced loneliness*** through Zoom or a number of other similar ways now set up. Often you can join just by pressing a link.

3. ***Avoid isolating yourself.*** I continually hear friends complaining that during these Covid-19 days their children will not "allow" them to leave their homes because of possible contagion. Carefully chosen socialization addresses an important need that television and streaming can't replace.

4. ***Grieving by yourself, cleaning house, repeatedly moping,*** screaming, and crying get pretty stale after several months. Put on your mask and gloves. Go shopping even if it's just online. Preferably, go outside. Many stores have instituted "senior" hours.

5. ***Bridge the death gap;*** select from cell phone photos of your loved one and form into a slide presentation that you can back with music.

6. ***Choose and delegate from among your friends*** those willing to listen, and provide emotional support; those who can offer more practical support; and avoid others who feel uncomfortable with grief. When invited out, pay your own way.

7. ***Recognize and be prepared for the ups and downs that come with grief.*** You'll have good days and bad days.

8. ***It's OK talking with your deceased spouse*** about your feelings, your loss and fears. With whom can you be more open?

9. ***Recognize how exhausted you are emotionally and physically.*** Rest and sleep are especially important in the early months.

10. ***Get out of the house.*** Take a drive. Walk in a park or around the block. Or even in a shopping center. Wear a mask and gloves. Avoid crowds but breathe free, even for a couple of hours.

CHAPTER V

MY COCOON BED

How many of us widows and widowers remember and yearn for the years of sleeping within a loved one's warm embrace? When Herb moved from our king-size bed into the nursing room and hospital bed it was a painful, wrenching transfer for both of us. I still sleep on my side in less than one-third of the bed, only enough to turn over as needed. At first, I tried to move at least half way to his side but the space was so open and empty I gave up.

I even laugh when it comes to changing the sheets because all I really need, but can't bring myself to do, is move to the fresh, other-side of the bed. It will still take time to recondition. Ingrained habits are difficult to change, especially at the beginning, so I remain with my nightly routine. A friend of mine changes her sheets only once every three weeks as she moves from segment to segment. But she has logged additional years of widowhood over me.

What's the Point?

Daily life follows a similar pattern. What's the point of cooking? The first week I boxed up all the cans and packages of foods that Herb enjoyed (and I didn't) and turned them over to a food bank. We'd rarely eaten the same foods over more recent years as his dietary needs and wants changed and it was always my pleasure to cater to him. Left to my own devices out went milk, bread, bananas, cake (the cookies I kept), most carbohydrates, and lots of other former basics. I now choose easy, one-course dishes that can last for a couple of days, including Costco rotisserie chicken that is useful either hot or cold. I often nibble on cold slices when I'm hungry and want fast protein. Fresh vegetables, when I'm ambitious enough to wash and chop them, converge in the form of salads. And I much prefer basic fish broiled with butter and lemon. Nothing fancy. No takeout. No bother. No fuss. No interest.

My daughter and grandson were shocked during a recent visit when they peeked into my empty refrigerator. I'd made a lovely dinner the night before to welcome them but there wasn't much in there other than left overs and the few additions I thought they might enjoy. Both decided to take me shopping at Trader Joe's. I declined explaining that the ice cream in the freezer, the cookies on the counter, and the cut class bowl by my computer filled with chocolate kisses were my preferred choices in eating. But if they looked in the downstairs freezer, they would find the formal foods, soups and meats now gathering ice waiting to be used. "I have exactly what I choose to eat," was my dismissal. And I mean it. The only time now that I use the dishwasher is when I have dinner company, a practice I reserve for rare visits from my children and friends. Otherwise, I'm perfectly happy with throw-away dishes. No wash. No fuss. And certainly not as much food.

Keeping a Daily Routine

One pattern I will not break or postpone is my hour of exercise early each morning while meditating to CNN. It's a routine adapted over the years from a Pilates instructor, yoga, personal trainer, and various fitness centers. I add weights every other day. When Herb became too ill to leave alone by himself, I changed to this at-home routine. My "24/7" home-care ladies used to laugh at my routine. Eventually they asked to join me but I declined, as I also did when my brother-in-law visited and wanted to be included. This hour belongs to me exclusively, seven days a week. Although I don't always find it inviting, and sometimes consider rebelling, it's a part of my being. My legs and body insist. Sometimes Loganberry the cat lies beside me on the mat but even he wouldn't dream of interfering.

I also depend upon a regular daily routine, as I did when Herb and I had our home office. Every morning I shower, dress, choose a somewhat decent outfit, and apply a limited amount of makeup. These steps help me retain my equilibrium. Each day involves a degree of planning the night before to assure some variety. I schedule tasks, include trips outside for limited shopping and errands, and even plug in some gardening (not too often) and/or reading on the patio during spring and summer. Were I to skip a day, linger in bed, hang around in pajamas, and not make even a short list of plans for the day, I'd be out of sorts and depressed. But there are also days when I make my choice to pull all the plugs. No one else knows or cares. Strangely now, there are few demands.

Nights are different. They are long and lonely, even longer because they begin earlier in the evening than when Herb was alive. As a child I used to consider it punishment going to bed when it was still light outside. That's changed. Often during summer months, I prefer the comfort of leaning back on my bed cushions and reading to sitting alone on a chair in the much larger family room waiting until it gets dark outside. Obviously, I'm alone either way but the pillows on the bed offer enveloping warmth and security and bring comfort to my cocoon. Sometimes Loganberry jumps up and joins me but most of the time he prefers to cocoon by himself downstairs.

The Sounds of Silence

As a long-time insomniac, especially now that I'm alone, I've asked friends and family not to call me after 9 p.m. so that I can settle down by myself. Even Rachel Maddow, Chris Cuomo and I have parted company because the harsh news accumulation of the day upsets me. When not engaged in Zoom meetings or the Great Lecture Plus series, my current choices range from a book of light fiction to Netflix streaming and even the Hallmark channel. Happy stories always end kindly and provide something gentle to think about as I drop off. And I often commune with Herb, watching the slide presentation on my iPad that I put together with his photos. Crying sometimes helps to cleanse the day.

And when I can't fall asleep, I revert to something I used to scoff at in earlier days: I often put on the tv with the remote turned low. This muzzled sound early in the morning or late at night is a soporific that induces sleep. A friend, Carol, talks about the sound differential. After longtime care for her dying spouse, she too finds this current silence and loneliness as irritants. Instead, she has installed Amazon's Alexa in her bedroom for adjusting lights and turning music on and off without getting out of bed. Other people I've interviewed agree but prefer Amazon's Echo. Neither of these devices can directly access 911, the universal emergency call number. To call the police or EMS requires connection to an intermediary device called Ooma Telo that will then facilitate the command.

Insecurity

Isolation is a new development that's led to feelings of insecurity in my own home especially after so many years of being a couple. I feel my vulnerability and awake to the slightest noises or movements. Often my sleep, when I do fall asleep, is broken up multiple times during the night, especially with sounds like someone is walking up the stairs. I recently discovered these thud movements come from my cat who likes to walk on the treadmill in my bedroom. I've asked Loganberry to confine his exercise to daytime. Aware of this emptiness, and my exposure, I now keep a can of hornet spray in my night table as a defense should there be an attack. I read somewhere that the spray has a blinding 20-foot range, which eases my isolation and attack fears. Of course, I would first have to figure out how to open the can, which would be a problem in the dark. Cans and bottle caps these days seem to require Herculean force just to open and seem rather impractical for emergency defense.

Bed Companions

Besides the cat, there are always other reasons to wake from a less than sound sleep, especially amber emergency alerts and storm warnings that come through cell phones. My sleep psychologist (yes, I've bitten that bullet too and sought help) suggested that I leave the cell phone downstairs since I also have a dependable house phone on the nearby night table. But nighttime reinforces my overall sense of loneliness. Mainly, I miss Herb's warm body. It took months at the beginning of our marriage to learn to sleep with him and contort our bodies comfortably and now it will probably take years to learn to sleep without him.

This psychologist also suggested that I cover the clocks but that seems illogical since her questionnaire was filled with time questions-- about when I went to bed, how long it took me to fall asleep, how many times I awoke, and how long these intervals of wakefulness continued. Life is filled with contradictions.

My iPad is also a good bed companion. I find it a great help watching Netflix or reading the NY TIMES news "Digest" at 3 or 4 a.m. when I'm unable to fall back to sleep following a bathroom break. The "Digest" takes almost an hour and often prompts an additional hour or more of slumber.

But I've also found another pursuit, something I've always known about but overlooked more recently. Keeping busy with projects, and interviewing others in similar situations, allows me to focus on something other than myself and actually gives me incentive to sometimes even sleep.

Lessons Learned

1. *Choose physical exercise*, even if you have to do it at home alone, or by walking. You'll be really surprised to experience how exercise can improve your mood and energy levels.

2. *Find courses, programs, even films that draw your attention.* Nights are usually far longer now than they were before your loss and can often drag on through the early hours. Netflix, Great Courses, and other streaming programs may carry a subscription fee but are more consistent and varied than the regular, at-night cable fare.

3. *Avoid relying on drugs and alcohol* to relieve emotional pain. You'll find that pain digs in even deeper once the drug has worn off.

4. *Distance your cell phone at night* to a different room

5. *Keep your bedroom darkened* to induce and maintain a deep sleep.

6. *Consider Amazon's Alexa Echo, Apple's Siri* or perhaps even *Google Assist* that may help you feel more secure and comfortable because they can connect voice-activated 911 emergency calls when paired with another device.

7. *Please yourself.* Choose foods, books, tv or other programs that bring you relaxation and comfort.

8. *Seek routine:* a comfortable schedule, consistency in dress, chores and activity that will pull you along even when you don't feel like it.

9. *Discover the world in miniature:* look at flowers, small animals, even insects that offer lives far beyond yours.

10. *Volunteer to do something for someone else* so that you're not always concentrating on yourself.

CHAPTER VI

LEGAL PANDEMONIUM

Years ago, I read some financial and legal recommendation that advised the survivor to empty out a bank vault immediately because on death these boxes are sealed. I doubt whether that advice was accurate for me, in particular, because the box was in my name only. But that was actually fortuitus advice. The day after Herb died, son Steve and I went to the bank and emptied out my strongbox. Because of the coronavirus, the bank locked up only hours after our visit. Although I had no money in the strongbox, there were papers that would be needed once I began switching beneficiaries, home titles, and even bank accounts. The bank itself took months to reopen, and only by special appointment. I would have been up a creek without those papers.

The funeral chapel ordered multiple copies (8) of Herb's death certificate for me. Because of closed offices, their advisor recommended that I allow as many as six weeks to receive these copies. I found this additional guidance exceptionally helpful, especially with a list of the immediate contacts I needed to make. The certificates came in eight weeks.

Nowhere in all this process did I realize that all incoming accounts involving both our names would freeze. Fortunately, our broker strongly advised that I transfer the equivalent of about four months of funding needs into our regular joint checking account. Since Herb had not written a check in recent years, it was the only financial group I chose not to inform. Nor have I updated the checking account because I like having his name on the checks. But the point is that fortunately I did have funds to draw upon for burial expenses, semi-annual property taxes, and emergency tree removal even when everything else was closed to me and awaiting transfer.

The Paperwork Curse--Proving My Existence

Every form was conditional on Herb's death certificate. Not even the brokerage would accept a cremation certificate, which I had in hand immediately. First, in order of priorities, was continued access to money. All incoming funds from our joint brokerage account, monthly social security payments and even Herb's monthly pension were now frozen until I could produce the death certificate. That policy seems to vary by area because a friend, Rae, simply used a notice from the funeral home and copy of the obituary to bypass most of what I dealt with.

Next came my notifications to life insurance companies, social security, and our pension fund. Although nothing could be completed without the death certificate there was no point delaying the volumes of paper work. It was again fortuitous that I had emptied out all kinds of legal papers from the safe deposit box because the demands for proof of our births, and marriage were mind-boggling. Metropolitan Life, although only a minimal policy, was the most demanding. North Western Mutual was amazingly responsive and fast. Their check was the first in. I will always be appreciative of their curtesy and promptness.

Now even the title of our home had to be changed solely to my name with another form to declare my children as my beneficiaries and avoid probate should I suddenly die. I'd made changes twice in previous years. The first was after Herb had his stroke and wasn't expected to live; and the second when things seemed brighter and I'd reversed that action. At those times there was no problem in completing the filings by myself. State and county offices were open and required limited effort to bring the corrected forms to a few offices for signatures and stamping. This time, because of the sequestering, I required legal assistance. The attorney charged $700, far more than I'd expected for under two hours of work. I made sure after that to handle the rest and not involve him further.

Social Security

Social Security was personified by one very nice lady working from home in Akron, Ohio, with a dog barking and a toddler cooing near her. Social Security required both my birth certificate and original marriage certificate before they would pay the one-time burial fee of $255. The lady promised to send me a stamped envelope for the transmission. The search for this certificate kept me awake for two nights and I was afraid I'd have to tell my three children that they were illegitimate.

I wondered whether the $255 from Social Security for death benefits was important enough to go through the long, frustrating effort of reincarnation for a marriage certificate I hadn't seen in 56+ years. But Herb's monthly Social Security payment was a horse of a different color. His payment was significantly larger than mine due to the missing ten years' I'd devoted to raising children. I resumed my search for the marriage certificate in earnest as I struggled to remember since it wasn't with the other papers. I found it folded inside a1963 newspaper photo and clipping of our wedding, all removed from that same safe deposit box. The certificate was punctually returned within just a couple of weeks.

I've since been surprised to find in my interviews that this missing wedding certificate can be a huge problem for others as well. Sharon, widowed just a year before this pandemic, had to contact Cuyahoga County to order a new copy because hers never showed up in other files and papers. The wedding certificate, and later my original Social Security card, turned out to be the most esoteric and the most critical because they had the potential for blocking everything else. Again, immediate replacement was almost impossible during Covid-19 because all state and county offices were closed with employees working from home.

The Pension

The real bane of my existence came from Herb's Pension-Benefits' Service Center. He and I had long ago agreed to accept a lower monthly payment from his former company, in Columbus, Ohio, so that I would be listed as his beneficiary and qualify for extension of his pension through my own lifetime. It wasn't a huge amount, but combined with Social Security added a nice cushion. That saga, all by itself, merits a separate chapter.

The Stimulus Payment

This stimulus step was supposed to be easy. It certainly was an extra, through unexpected payment. The U.S. government does not often give money away but with Covid-19, and this current tailspin economy, $1200 payment per adult was supposed to be a layup--assuming that I met financial criteria, which I did. Herb and I had filed jointly each year from the beginning of our marriage. We were legitimate, so what could be difficult? Surprise.

Apparently, the Treasury Department changed its mind midstream and disallowed those who had died in the course of these payments. O.K., so we were down to one payment? Not even that one. Determined to find out why I'd received no payment or communication, I decided to bite the bullet and one day in July '20 I remained on hold awaiting a response from the IRS for two and a half hours. The kind voice explained that the government did not know specifically how to deal with the death of a joint filer and, therefore, withheld payment also from the survivor. The stimulus payment would supposedly be available as a claim deduction the following April 2021 when I filed my 2020 tax return. Apparently, my call made some headway and a month later found the $1200 electronically deposited into my checking account.

What Now

At the end of the first three months following Herb's death most incoming funds still remained frozen. I found myself with only the money I had transferred to my checking account, still awaiting the Social Security death benefit of $255, brokerage account access, Social Security monthly payment, insurances, and the most challenging void of all, Herb's pension. Who knew how long these financial readjustments would take? Fortunately, I still could draw from our one checking account that remained accessible to me. I sometimes wonder how Herb might have managed were he the surviving spouse but, giving credit where it's due, Herb was always quick to catch on (although in earlier years before his stroke he sometimes forgot even to write down on the tab the few deductions for checks he might have written).

Ignorance, A Frequent Excuse

These initial steps to widowhood indeed do try men's and women's souls. Even worse encounters await those who are totally ignorant of their joint or separate spouses' finances. Too many catastrophes result from this lack of knowledge or preparation, including being unaware of whom to trust for guidance.

Talking with other widows and widowers I've been surprised, even flabbergasted, to find how many chose not to be involved in the details underlying their marriages and finances. I spoke recently to a friend of my husband's (from early days). The four of us had been in touch over the years and Joyce called to see how I was getting along in these early months of widowhood. I shared some of my financial frustrations with her.

Joyce

Joyce reported that her late husband had done all the banking, check paying, insurances and investments. When she asked that Saul share some of this responsibility he often demurred by saying, "You have so many other things to do. Let me worry about these." Or he would choose a time late in an evening when she was too tired to deal with any of these details. When he died suddenly nine years ago, her daughter-in-law stepped forward to educate her about the check book and other forms of fiscal management. Both her son and daughter-in-law continue to provide guidance as needed.

The upshot was, however, that Joyce was really surprised to learn that it only took her six weeks or so to grab the essentials. She reminded me of my own father who had never made out a check or balanced an account until my mother died at age 52. He was forced from necessity to figure it out by himself, as he did the washing machine, too.

"He takes care of me," not always the protection one assumes, can backfire. Other spouses may become totally dependent on their late spouse's co-workers or designated executor to handle business issues. When financial matters are relegated to a business partner, relative or attorney, spouses too often discover that not all executors are trustworthy.

On the other hand, Sheila was in complete charge of the family's finances, including income taxes, and she thinks Michael might have had some challenges were he to have been the surviving spouse. Keeping good records and a filing system is key for the subsequent health and wellbeing of the survivor. But this responsibility must be shared and communicated between both spouses. Some of us need to readjust our thinking and planning because we tend to be arrogant about this responsibility. We need make sure that our survivor is not set adrift without an oar. Vicki, found out by reading an annual report of missing state funds in the local Cleveland newspaper that several thousand dollars held in her late husband Marty's name were due her from insurance reimbursements.

Marcia

Marcia's husband, a financial analyst, held all the financial records and legal documents together in a special loose-leaf file "with a white cover." Because of his knowledge and administrative skills, he served as executor for multiple family members. The only problem was that he died unexpectedly at their winter home in Sarasota, Florida, and the loose-leaf file remained in Boston and initially out of view because Marcia remained with her daughter for some period. But eventually everything was found in good order. But it took a while to pull it all together.

Marcia has a trusted financial advisor selected by her late husband who is there to guide her in investments and financial decisions.

Sharon

Much too often, it's the spouse in charge of the "papers" who dies unexpectedly and inconveniently. Another problem experienced by Sharon following her husband's sudden death was the search for the family's funeral plot records. The synagogue, founded by Jerry's family, had closed and the cemetery did not have any plot numbers specifically listed under her name. Compounding the search and time pressures, her husband Jerry had never shared the location where he'd filed the papers. It took many anguished hours by frantic family members to locate "the envelope." Her son eventually found it in a closet filed with unrelated business papers.

Cindy

Cindy had most of her financial records in order but encountered a different problem. Although her late husband had retired from his position, he still dabbled in consulting for a few selected clients and, as she later discovered, kept a separate but relatively small account in his own name. She needed legal support to retrieve these funds now caught in probate. His regular attorney and friend relegated her file to a younger staff member in his law firm who stalled and delayed over an entire year, routinely sending costly billings but providing little attention.

"Make sure you're on the same level in communicating with your lawyer," advises Cindy. She later found it necessary to review all of her insurances previously overseen by her husband as well as to change insurance agents when she discovered that her house was overvalued. The long relationship between the insurance agent and her husband excluded Cindy and she personally felt turned off by the agent's lack of effort to make any meaningful connection with her, even failing to make a personal call to acknowledge her husband's passing. Surviving spouses, especially those who newly assume financial responsibility, can often be taken for granted as well as overcharged. Cindy subsequently changed agencies at a substantial cost savings.

Lessons Learned

1. ***Know your finances.*** Too many husbands, even in the 21st century, consider their life-long mission is to "protect" their wives by freeing them from the incumbrances and inconveniences of learning about banking, investments, credit accounts, home ownership, and budgets. "Protect the Little Lady" seems to be an ill-conceived theme.

2. ***Organize and update all important documents.*** Know not only your immediate finances but also any separate accounts that may not be available to you by joint signature.

3. ***Learn!*** Too many widows and widowers have never used a check book or ever talked to their financial consultant or stock broker.

4. ***Be aware of all information*** about an updated will, divorce settlements, designated beneficiaries and executor, legal power of attorney, and medical powers of attorney.
5. ***Make sure stock and property holdings are updated in both your names*** to avoid probate.
6. ***File important papers in one secure place for safe keeping and retrieval.***[11] These include:
   - Funeral arrangements
   - Wills and trusts, both yours and your spouse's.
   - Birth and marriage certificates (yours and your spouse's)
   - Original notarized wedding certificate (a religious certificate doesn't count)
   - Original social security cards for both of you (you can reorder from Social Security)
   - Pension and retirement plans
   - Tax returns
   - Investment accounts
   - Deeds
   - Loan statements
   - Divorce agreements
   - Funeral plots
   - Life insurance policies
   - Health insurance
   - Loans
   - Property titles, mortgages, deeds, leases
   - Car insurance, motor vehicle titles
   - Homeowner's insurance
   - Health insurance
   - Names of attorney, accountant, broker and executor
   - Checkbooks, personal savings and business accounts, CDs, and anything else pertinent to your finances
   - Outstanding bills
   - Safe deposit box information (and location)
   - Business ownership or interest

---

11   Marcia shared a concise listing from Balance, a financial fitness program, that rounded out my own list.

- Military service records
- Computer records related to assets.

7. ***Create a digital version of important papers for easy storage and accessibility.*** Banks, vaults, government offices may close during pandemics; even houses can burn down; hard drives can blow up; lawyers and accountants can retire. *Evernote* is a handy computer tool in our paperless society that will keep all this vital information together, on line, and immediately available to both you and those whom you designate.

8. ***In advance maintain your own credit card(s) and credit history.*** List your utility bills in joint names or your own. Changing utilities and establishing credit at your stage of life is more than cumbersome.

9. ***Be familiar with your budgetary needs*** unless you prefer to designate someone to dole out an allowance to you weekly or monthly.

10. ***Avoid surprises.*** It's a good idea for your beneficiaries to know while your spouse is still alive the details of the estate and how funds will be shared or awarded.

CHAPTER VII

A PENSION OXYMORON

The most difficult of all my money transfers and funding sources involved Herb's pension from "B" Institute. Herb had worked at this non-profit think tank, in Columbus, Ohio, for eleven years, from 1967 to 1978, long enough to qualify for a small pension. Filling out his application forms when he resigned, we together agreed to accept a lower monthly payment in return for my listing as beneficiary were I to outlive Herb.

I contacted their pension service on April 4 to report Herb's passing the day before and was told there would be follow up. Nothing happened until June 4th, when I discovered an online debit of the same amount to my checking account reversing their May '20 payment. [12]There was no explanation for this debit. I realized then that, absorbed in the midst of all this other activity, I'd heard nothing from the pension fund during these 2 ½ months.

The Saga Begins

Calling the same number printed on a receipt from a previous pension payment, I was routed to a woman, in Boston and working from home, who informed me that my "grieving" packet had been delayed because of some "in-house" glitches but was on its way. It arrived a few days later and I immediately filled out and returned the forms along with copies, as required, with our required birth certificates, his death certificate and my social security card. This latter was the most difficult to locate. Like many of you of similar vintage, I had no idea where my original card was. I'd applied for that card as a pre-teenager, more than 70 years

---

12   I opted to close our consulting business and begin Herb's pension in July '01 following his massive stroke. For these 19+ years the pension was electronically deposited in our joint checking account monthly. Obviously their benefits company was familiar with both who we were and how to access our account. No surprises.

before. After assigning that number to my indelible memory forever, I'd filed and forgotten it through all the moves and changes in my life.

I vaguely remembered ordering a replacement card, in 1963, to reflect my new name when Herb and I married. Wonder of wonders, I found that second card in a long-neglected lock box in my bedroom closet, tucked into an envelope along with Herb's and our children's social security cards. I copied the more recent card and on June 9 sent it along with all the other required enclosures to the address I was given using my own large manilla envelope. No self-addressed envelope was provided in my "grief" packet.

I followed up again within several days to my new friend working at home in Boston to assure the pension service had received my packet. She told me that my copy of the social security card was unacceptably blurred[13] and the pension service had denied my application. I asked to speak with a supervisor but was told none was available. Nor did any return my call. It was time for a rejoinder and, yes, I was angry. It was time to take my complaint to the top, to the director of this subcontractor for whom there was no name.

June 8, 2020
Director
Pension Service Center

Dear Person of Authority:
I wish to report how displeased I am with your entire processing. My comments deal with the following:
- *Your archaic computer system that loses grief packets.*
- *The requirement that I provide a copy of my original social security card and number. I haven't used that card in 70+ years. Not even Social Security itself required this copy to transfer accounts.*
- *Your packet did not include a return envelope.*

Your handling of this pension transfer does not instill a feeling of confidence.

---

13   The copy was perfectly clear as attested by a second copy I'd also made.

The Pension Service, Des Moines, Iowa, responded with a second form letter.

June 15, 2020

Dear Berenice E. Kleiman:
The B Pension Service Center[14] has received your paperwork. Unfortunately, the paperwork you submitted is missing information that is required in order for the PSC to complete the processing. We have noted below in the Issues and Next Steps, highlighted in italics, you need to resolve the outstanding issues....You did not send the required documentation. Please send the Pension Service Center a legible copy of your Social Security Card.... We cannot process your payment until we receive the documentation outlined above....

In other words, they rejected my pension application.[15] I knew the copy of my card was absolutely legible because I'd double-checked it before enclosing it in my own manila envelope with other forms to the pension center. I called again, reached the same clerk in Boston, and asked once again to speak to a supervisor. "Not available," I was told, "But she would leave a message."

On June 18, in utmost frustration, I directed the following letter to the President and CEO of "B" Institute, Herb's former employer.

June 18, 2020

President & CEO

---

14 I've chosen not to identify this company by direct name.

15 I've since questioned many friends and contacts of similar vintage to see if they still have access to their original Social Security cards. Only those aged 40 and younger appear to have some connection to their card. Those of my vintage were cautioned when young to avoid identify fraud by never carrying this card in our wallets.

Dear Mr. ----:

My husband Dr. Herbert S. Kleiman was on your staff, in Columbus, for 11 years, from 1967-1978 and earned a small pension for which I was designated as his beneficiary. Herb died on April 3, 2020 and I have been wrangling with your pension company ever since. After informing them of my husband's death on April 4, I heard nothing until I saw a "pre-authorized debit" on my checking account of $_____ on June 4th. In response to my query, your Pension Service Center told me that the delay of their condolence packet was because of "systemic problems". It arrived on June 6 with the strange requirement that I provide an original copy of my social security card and number. I haven't used that card in 70 years but after much searching, I did find, copy and enclose a 1963 replacement, along with the completed forms and an accompanying cover letter of complaint I'd sent them for their slowness both in communicating and requiring this archaic piece of ID.

With no response I finally called the Pension Service Center today and discovered that they have rejected a full-page copy of my little card for unknown reasons. They are scrambling now to determine why.

Mr. ____, I hope this Chinese torture is not how your company regularly treats its widows. This pension isn't much really. I don't think it will sacrifice what's left of your portfolio. But it would be helpful to me. Further, I don't think your pension service is serving your interests or the interests of your aging employees and their spouses.

Sincerely,
Berenice E. Kleiman
Encl: June 8th letter to B's outsourced Pension Service Center

My letter broke the log jam. Within days, a call came from "B's" Benefits consultant, Joan, in Columbus, who showed compassion for my loss and apologized for the treatment I'd received. She had both my letters, to "M" and "B", on her desk and promised to follow through. Just two hours later, Niles, a supervisor from the Benefits Center, called to say I would receive the missing May, June and July payments by July 14. Regularly scheduled pension payments in my name would then begin on August 1st.

I told this supervisor that I required a confirming letter restating this information. I also raised three additional questions: 1) Why it took so long to get a supervisor's response; 2) Why a special exception was being made in my case when all "B" spouses should have the right to prompt attention and options for fulfillment; and 3) Why an original Social Security card was even required as the only acceptable identification? He sputtered, unable to answer these questions. I later also raised the same questions directly with Joan, at "B" but never received an answer from either them.

The Logjam Still Didn't Break

"B" company was now aware of my problems and poor performance by their new pension center, to which they'd changed from in-house fulfillment about a year before. The pension center subsequently reconfirmed that I would receive retroactive payments by July 14 with regular monthly payments beginning on August 1, 2020.

By July 14, watching my checking account online all day, I became well aware that there was no deposit from B. At 9 p.m. that evening I received a called from "Darwin" in Dallas telling me the payments were still being processed and were on route. I questioned why he was calling so late and what "on route" meant since we had just passed the deadline set by his company. He promised to check. On July 15, the next morning, I received a call from "Maegan," in Michigan, as well as a second from someone at "M", who said she was responding to my July 2nd request for a supervisor. At that point I told her I would no longer respond to anyone from "M", the subcontractor, and immediately emailed Joan, the benefits supervisor at "B", telling her I'd had it with the gang who couldn't shoot straight.

Joan phoned me immediately to report that "M" had mailed a check to me through the post office on what they claimed was July 2.

Obviously, I hadn't received this mailing for these ten business days. She offered to stop payment on the check and have this service company issue another check. Since that would involve another two weeks or longer, especially the way they kept time, my email response to her was:

July 14, 2020

Why would "M" send me a live check when they already have been posting monthly deposits to Herb's and my joint checking account for decades? And why would they not inform me of the status of this check? Also, what was the purpose of their call last night? "Darwin" wasn't even sure what he was supposed to tell me.

This company, "M", seems so totally incompetent that I am amazed they can support so many different office locations. Or that "B" would use their services. How many other "B" widows have been caught in this morass?

I told Joan that enough was enough. I required "M" to electronically deposit the back payments into my account within two days, by Friday, July 17. And I promised to tear up the laggard check should the mail arrive after the deposit. It did so on the following Saturday, one week later.

The Battle Continues

On Friday afternoon, I followed up with a (hopefully) concluding email to "B" informing the benefits manager that the first part—the three-month payment in arrears—had arrived but only by electronic deposit.

July 17, 2020

Dear Joan,

At 7:03 a.m. this Friday morning 7/17/20 the missing 3-month pension deposit finally appeared electronically in my online banking account. I delayed my response to you until mail delivery today, at 12:50, so I could report that the snail mail did NOT arrive. You are now free to cancel/revoke the previous check.

Again, I do not know how your "M" could have possibly screwed things up as badly and continuously. I do know, however, that I have gone through three and a half months of steady aggravation and frustration. At first it was funny to witness the confusion on their part. And then it wasn't. I specifically thank you for stepping in to try to correct what should have been an easy transfer of beneficiary when they had all the paperwork and directives from the beginning.

I think it's only fair that "B" or "M" replace the 10 pounds of Hershey's milk chocolate kisses that I've eaten during this period to keep my sanity. There is a big, empty crystal bowl next to my computer table that requires refilling. I would also like letters of apology from both your company and this benefits company with whom you've subcontracted. And, finally, I would like your word that other widows and widowers will have options to prove their identity rather than simply "an original" Social Security card.

Sincerely yours,
Berenice E. Kleiman

I emailed the following to "B":

July 22

Joan,

To tell you the truth, the envelope with Saturday, July 18th arrival lay on my desk unopened until now. My intent as promised was to shred it but I simply wasn't up to opening this up until two minutes ago. To my astonishment, it simply contained another acknowledgement that the "B" check "was delivered to my home address." It also stated that there were 3 tax exemptions—news to me. The remaining sheet of paper was blank.

THIS CHECK WAS NOT ENCLOSED! THERE HAS BEEN NO CHECK MAILED TO MY ADDRESS BEFORE, DURING OR AFTER OUR COMMUNICATIONS!! AND BESIDES I HAVE ONLY 1 EXEMPTION.

Joan, I leave this in your hands. I can only hope that on August 1st I receive the first of regular beneficiary payments delivered electronically to my checking account. Frankly, I don't want to know anymore.

Sincerely,
Berenice E. Kleiman

Yes, There's still more

July 25, 2020

Joan,

The "B" check finally arrived by snail mail today, Saturday, July 25. It was dated July 3. With your knowledge and permission, I will shred it. Thank you for all your help in resolving this very difficult situation. But I would still like to speak with your superior on Monday.

Berenice

The first regular "B" pension payment was electronically deposited to my checking account on Friday, August 1st, but not before I received another communication from "M" stating that I would need to complete a beneficiary form, again by snail mail. I tore that up.

August 1

Dear Joan and Dave [her boss],

The first in the new series of Herb Kleiman's regularly scheduled pension payments was deposited electronically this morning to my checking account. I sincerely appreciate the effort made by both of you to dislodge this payment from M.

However, I am not about to call it a day until I receive the two requests I have made to your subcontractor: 2 letters of apology and the Hershey's milk chocolate kisses. I feel it is only appropriate for them to acknowledge the stress and frustration they subjected me to over four months based on their carelessness and poor management. Their behavior is particularly inexcusable because of the pain thrust upon me as a new widow.

Again, my thanks to "B" and to both of you for stepping in to make things right--something that should have been done by "M" from the very beginning.

Sincerely,
Berenice Kleiman

August 2, 2020

Dear Berenice, thank you for this update. We are both very happy to see resolution and appreciate your feedback.

As I mentioned during our call, the level of quality of service is something that falls to me to uphold, and I sincerely apologize for your experience. While we will discuss with "M" a written apology, we cannot provide you with the requested chocolates, and will not request this from "M". It sets a precedent and process that we cannot replicate. I second my apology specifically in terms of the stress this situation has caused you.

Dave D.
Director of Benefits
B. Institute"

August 3, 2020

Dave,

Apology accepted. Thank you. My hope is that "B" will more closely monitor "M" so that this insensitive response to pension applicants does not reoccur.

Berenice

Belated Response from a "M" "Supervisor"

August 6,

Dear Ms. Kleiman,

As the "M" Client Relationship Leader for "B", Institute, I am writing to personally apologize for your experience with our pension administration services since being notified of your husband's passing.

    Dave D. has shared with me the details of what has transpired over the past 4 months, and I must say the stress and frustration you have had to endure as a new widow is inexcusable. I assure you that we are taking the necessary steps to prevent something like this from ever happening in the future.

At "M", one of our core values is, "we treat others the way we want to be treated." I'm very sorry that we did not meet this standard in your personal situation.
If you have any further questions or would like to discuss this matter further, please feel free to contact me at my personal number __ at any time.

Sincerely,

————,
Client Relationship Leader

August 6

Dear Mr.____:

I appreciate your apology and, in particular, the steps "M" is taking to preclude the four-month series of errors and disassociations that blocked efforts to retrieve my husband's pension. Had I had your name as Client Relationship Leader for "B" in response to my numerous requests for "a person in authority," it would not have been necessary to contact "B" directly.

I hope that no subsequent widow or widower is subjected to this ugly and unfortunate exercise. Should you have any questions or prefer to discuss this matter further, you may contact me at 216----.

Sincerely,
Berenice E. Kleiman

And We Move On

Grieving requires tremendous will to fight our way to fulfillment. It shouldn't be necessary to hire an attorney to cut through these obstacles, although an attorney's letterhead might have prompted a faster response from the pension service. But even that would not bridge the gap to cover the missing social security card or this company's sheer stupidity.

At least this part of the battle did have value. I've since been informed by "B" that the qualification requirement for the "original" Social Security card has since been extended to include other options for identification.

I didn't start out to be an activist. But, it still boggles my imagination to realize how many obstacles, hurdles and glitches are thrust upon widows and widowers during this time of great loss. Pandemic confusion does not excuse disinterest, inertia or perhaps even an intention to delay payment. Apologies, yes, but alas no chocolates.

The amount of this pension didn't sink my battleship but it certainly could sink someone else's. I'm grateful to "B"[16] and their in-house Benefits Department and sincerely hope this limited experience has helped them rethink their relationship with this outsourced pension service. And yes, I can live without the chocolates but it would have been a soothing conciliatory step for either or both companies to make.

LESSONS LEARNED

1. *Expect to keep certain financial records forever.*
2. *Duplicate your paper base electronically.* Marriage licenses, social security cards, birth certificates, insurance policies, corresponding amendments, wills, letters, titles should all be kept in separate labeled envelopes in a vault or security box. Or online.
3. *File all copies of importance under both Dropbox and Evernote,* in your computer system.
4. *Share the locations of both paper and electronic storage with your designated executor* should you suddenly die.
5. *Encourage your grown children to do the same.*
6. *Be willing to fight for an injustice,* especially a monetary one that is unquestionably yours.

---

16   I've chosen to hide both company names. We live in a litigious society and I've obviously had enough difficulty obtaining the pension and prefer not to lose it. But the difficult case was made and the pension is now regularly deposited.

7. ***Go right to the top of an organization to get satisfaction.***
   As my father taught me many years ago, they and their
   representatives are the only ones who may respond.
8. ***Make copies of all correspondence and follow-up***,
   including names, dates and times for the people with whom
   you've spoken.
9. ***Never throw out a "money" file.*** Organize and date all
   records and correspondence because you never know when
   you're going to have to resurrect and prove ownership.
10. ***Sometimes anger and frustration provide an unexpected
    diversion from grief. But why should this be necessary?***

CHAPTER VIII

THE DIFFERENCE BETWEEN BEING ALONE AND LONELINESS

Some time ago in discussion, a divorced friend, Miguel, introduced an issue about how he saw a wide difference between being alone and lonely. He explained that he welcomed being alone and living without the rancor that had flowed through his previous marriage. But being lonely raised another issue for him as his walls at home sometimes ring with silence.

I'd never thought much about either term but this distinction frequently occupies my thoughts now. As a lifelong "loner" I'd wrestled with that issue long before I met Herb. I especially remember a day late in my freshmen year at Syracuse University walking through Thorndon Park, near my small dorm, and pondering whether to declare for a sorority or remain independent. It was pretty obvious that the sororities were the way to "belong" on campus. But, for me, just joining one for its own sake would not work. The sororities I wanted had no similar need for me and those who might, just might, have put in a vote for me would not have worked. I chose to remain an independent and never regretted that decision.

The Loneliness of Losing Your Soulmate

Marriage was another step I agonized over and sometimes had fearful dreams that I would wake up on my honeymoon realizing I'd made a mistake. The question again loomed through my early twenties about whether it was wiser to form a "not quite fitting" relationship or risk never having that opportunity again. I chose again to take my chances, continued my education, and found both the husband and the career I wanted.

Herb and I, two transplanted New Yorkers, stumbled into each other in Baltimore when neither of us was recruiting. He had just taken a new position in a new city. I was living there, teaching and going to law school at the University of Maryland's downtown evening division, doing exactly what I wanted. It didn't take long. We were engaged in three months and married in seven.

Living with Herb for almost six decades found us both well anchored within our marriage. I can't say it was always ideal but it was good. Herb and I respected each other's need for space, matched intellectual drive, and pursued both similar and separate areas of interest. While not Siamese twins we were joined physically, emotionally, and, as I said in his eulogy, by the heart.

Widowhood, compounded by a pandemic, brings loneliness to the nth degree. Much as I enjoy my own time, and have overflowing independence (no more medical issues, schedules, therapies, crises, or emergency rooms), I miss Herb, our hugs, discussion and shared personhood. I especially miss this "sharing." Often now when I read an article or hear a discussion of mutual interest, I want to turn to Herb and tell him about the news. My cat has no such interest in politics.

The Danger of Isolation

As independent as I think I am, I recognize the danger of isolation. With the coronavirus spreading, I know many people who prefer the safety of six feet of separation, along with masks and hiding behind closed doors. Abject loneliness doesn't suit me. I need the stimulation of other people, especially those who are alive, bright and curious,

I spent the first summer and fall holding "high tea" on my patio outside under the red umbrella and inviting selected friends, often one at a time, for tea and conversation in mid-afternoon. Guests were free to bring whatever made them comfortable. One friend brought her own chair and thermos drink. Another brought her husband. It was fun getting to know both of them. Some wear masks. Some don't. It's really free-wheeling and provides a nice lift to the day. On extra hot or rainy days, I lured guests out of the sun into my air-conditioned family room while still observing the rules encouraging six feet of separation.

My practice on early weekends was to pursue some of the exploration that son Steve taught me. Often, I was delighted to drive some 40 minutes northeast to the Mentor Headlands for rest and recuperation. Herb and I used to visit it years ago, long before it became impossible to push his wheelchair through the sand. While I have no interest in going into the water, I loved to sit on a blanket, people and boat watch, read, or just reflect on life. This part of being alone is enjoyable and refreshing. Often, I'd stop at a favorite seafood restaurant on the way home and sit at an outside table by myself. My friend, Michael, was the only one willing to join me. I also hoped to inveigle him into hiking in nearby parks. We did some but not enough of that. Others usually cancel at the last minute because of heat or worries about crowds. Northern Ohio's cold winter weather has put a damper to these pleasant breaks.

Being Fearful

I hesitate to do out-of-the-way jaunts by myself even though I assume most places in this area have a cell phone signal in case of an emergency. I've become cautious about being alone in an isolated area in case I might fall. This experience was the first of two events that happened last summer in my own back yard. I'd been sitting on a lawn chair when the phone rang. Returning to my chair, I suddenly tripped over a backless pair of old, sloppy, shoes I was wearing and fell down, without blocking, hard on the grass directly on my nose and forehead. The whole thing came as a huge shock, especially since my balance is good. Or at least I used to think so.

I lay on the ground knowing that I'd crashed really hard and might have a concussion. I didn't try to get up for a matter of minutes. After a while, when I could, I took inventory and slowly pulled myself up and made my way inside to the kitchen. Before even opening the freezer for the ice tray I dumped those shoes into the garbage. Applying copious ice packs on my face and the bleeding bridge of my nose, I knew I had dodged a bullet.

Later fluorescent streams of light streaked from the corner of my right eye. I struggled for hours to stay awake and not give into fear. While there was no point in calling EMS, the fall was a jolt, making me realize that I was truly on my own. For the first time I felt truly vulnerable. When Herb was so badly disabled, I still felt in control. During these 20 years, I'd survived shingles, flu and even a kidney stone without calling for help. Now being hurt and alone was a new issue. Headaches continued for a couple of weeks and the big bruise on my nose was pretty obvious, especially on Zoom conferences. People were generally too polite to question although I was quite prepared to blame the attack on Loganberry.

Self-Protection

Three weeks later, and still within the first three months of widowhood, I tripped over an elastic band on the corner of the air mattress I use for exercising and went flying three feet into the wall. My head banged against the wall and I heard a sharp crack. Again, I lay there until I could collect myself and take inventory.

My first response was relief as I stretched arms, legs and then my hips. Although I'd hit the right side of my head really hard, nothing seemed broken. It took time to pull myself up. And again, I felt relief that I'd dodged another bullet. But two falls in three weeks are a cause for concern even when I don't consider myself awkward or unbalanced.

This second fall snapped me out of the smugness I've felt watching some friends of similar age using crutches and pushing walkers. Because of years of exercise I'm not someone who falls and my balance is generally pretty good. But yes, the fluorescent streaks were still there. Fortunately, through friends, I was able to arrange an appointment with a retina specialist within three days. I've subsequently had laser eye surgery to avoid a continuing and expanding tear in the retina of my right eye and will be followed closely to assure this tear does not spread. Both the fluorescents and tracers remain but to a lesser degree. My vision may never be the same.

When sharing this experience, my friend's response was "Why didn't you call me?" That was followed by "Why didn't you go to the emergency room?" Neither choice was a consideration. But worry is now planted about what I will I do the next time should I need help?

I chose not to discuss either of these falls or my associated concerns with my children. They have their own lives and I do not want them to think of me as "the little mother" in need of their protection. And at this point in time, I still prefer not to wear a bell or buzzer.

Now in my early '80s, both events coming so closely force me to wonder about future years. And I worry about an out-of-the-blue illness, especially with Covid-19 so rampant, or even the next accident. Will another incapacitate me and rob me of my independence? As with Herb and too many of our friends, I've watched how accidents and illnesses come on suddenly and rob us of our decision making. Were I to fall down the basement steps, suffer a stroke, or, yes, even be attacked, *I am alone.* And I know it. While I don't feel I'm ready to wear that buzzer or bell, this kind of being "alone" in early widowhood is truly perplexing. I'd like to think that these two random circumstances will not repeat, *but what happens if they do?*

In my Medical Power of Attorney instructions, I decline any end-of-life interruptions, including resuscitation and ventilators. I've communicated these wishes to my medical power of attorney designee—Steve-- directly. Since Steve is not here and is frequently traveling, I've asked my local friend, Michael, to be my medical power of attorney as I will be his. Fortunately, he is a physician and formerly for many years my internist. Unfortunately, directions are not always followed. My precious independence raises the prospect that were I unable to speak up for myself there may be no one who can easily come to my assistance. Few people are aware that I have a life threatening, adverse reaction to ALL medications. This fear of aloneness certainly underscores the dark side of widowhood.

A psychologist friend of mine advised me that when three falls within a limited period are recorded, authorities make every effort to begin steering that person to an assisted living facility. Obviously, I plan to double my flamingo/yoga leg lift exercises, which I do whenever I stop to fill up my gas tank. In the meantime, I have no plans to communicate these falls to my current internist.

Thinking About Getting a Dog

I've discovered another factor about pandemics. Because so many people are now working or hovering at home, the U.S. has experienced a run on toilet paper, bicycles, and even shelter dogs, particularly the small, cuddly breeds. As one who has always had dogs and, more recently, cats, I yearn to rekindle the early morning walks I used to take with my dogs. Googling a list of area dog shelters within a 50-mile radius, I emailed each one with my request for a small, house-broken, non-shedding dog. Most of these offices have remained closed with people working from home. Those who did respond reported that small dogs are quickly snatched up, often by people doing foster care for the same dogs. Only the mastiffs and pit bulls with huge snouts remain available. While some of these may be sweethearts in disguise, I've promised my cat that I will not bring home any animal larger than his 15 pounds. Loganberry was an intimidated rescue cat seven years ago when removed from a home with three large dogs. Here he rules the roost.

The only other opportunity seems to be starting again with a puppy who has a 10-14+ year lifespan and would more than likely outlive me. Both the cost and this long-life concern are unappealing. The last time I checked, the on-line quote for a miniature schnauzer puppy was $5200 plus a $750 "transportation" fee. For a while it looked like Loganberry and I would remain a two-some. Loganberry aware of my conversations with animal shelters has since become much more accommodating and affectionate, especially in the evenings when I hate being alone.

News

But strange, unexpected developments do occur. Early in October I took possession of a 10-week-old Corgi puppy I named Winston (Winnie) as in Winston Churchill's nickname. Since the Queen of England has her Corgi dogs I thought it would be both fitting and proper to remain within the British theme. The debate was whether to instead call him Harry, as in Prince Harry, because of the similarity in tawny coloring.

Having a puppy after so many years became an awesome challenge, beginning again with teething, toilet training, and convincing

Loganberry that a little brother could be fun. And perhaps his presence will fill even just a little of my loneliness…and keep me jumping and energized with new, fresh challenges. Even though others may frown on the "work" involved, I welcomed the loving distraction, at least most of the time.

Lessons Learned

1. **Exercise regularly** to move your body and retain balance.
2. **Find "safe" outings** that you know and enjoy.
3. **Invite friends to share** these outings but also feel free to go by yourself.
4. **Discard clumpy old shoes.**
5. **Consider wearing a button to summon help** when you begin to feel concerned for your welfare
6. **Organize surprises and unusual boosts to the day** and week that you enjoy.
7. **Figure out what energizes and invigorates you.**
8. **Take walks, drives, even visits to stores during less crowded times.** Some stores offer special senior hours.
9. **Research to find interesting places** within a limited radius that remain open. Bring a picnic lunch.
10. **Consider "high tea" with friends.** It's really comforting when they begin to return the invitations.

CHAPTER IX

ARE YOU PLANNING TO SELL YOUR HOUSE?

Many people, even with the best of intensions, fail to realize how intrusive their questions are. Or how much these questions really hurt. Maybe they do, which may be why so many withdraw and hide from you after their initial onslaught. Until they themselves face a similar challenge, they probably will not be cognizant of the sharpness or discomfort raised by their questioning.

The House is Empty

Even with a 20-year advance, my house and heart are empty. Poor Loganberry still mopes around searching for his buddy. Suddenly, the man who'd occupied the center of my existence, my best friend and soulmate is gone, along with his hospital bed, wheelchair, cases of Depends, pads, meds, pyramid walker and braces, commode, and recliner. Also missing are his unconquerable spirit, and personality.

Loads of wash from bedclothes remained immediately after the 24/7 team departed. None of that work required thought, only stamina. The chairlift remained busily reoccupied conveying up baskets of clean sheets and towels, adding a welcome distraction to putting everything back in their proper places. But the medical equipment remained. It was hard to give away equipment, including multiple wheelchairs and walker. The same charitable companies that used to send monthly postcards soliciting contributions now no longer encourage even drop-offs because of fear of Covid-19 contagion.[17] Equipment, including

---

17   Purple Heart and other non-profit organizations were not eager to pick up clothing and equipment from homes these days because of Covid-19. But I did find a religious organization that removed all of the medical equipment and supplies for distribution to people in need. They also suggested to me that I retain one of everything, from wheelchair to shower-bench and walker for a future time when I may have to use them myself. So, the former "hospital room" is now a holding pen

five wheelchairs, remained piled up both in the closed bedroom and in the garage. And I haven't even begun to think about Herb's clothing.

Keeping a Sense of Humor

On top of the dining room buffet sits the maroon and silver urn with Herb's ashes and his small framed photo perched above. A few people flinch uncomfortably when I point this out. Obviously, some think it macabre. I find Herb's closeness comforting. I promised him I'd never leave him alone. I myself view a cemetery open to all-weather elements as intimidating, cold and lonely. Herb and I never liked large crowds. And, yes, we agreed in advance to this plan.

But so many others whom I've interviewed also admit to being especially rankled by similar questions directed from well-meaning friends, relatives and neighbors. I've earlier shared my flip reaction to the hospice nurse's uncomfortable pushing. Her reaction taught me to remain guarded in further responses.

The Questions People Ask

"How are you?" people ask when saying hello. How should I respond?
- *Wiped out.*
- *Sad.*
- *Depressed*
- *Empty*
- *Lonely*
- *Yearning for one more hour or one more day, and night, with my husband*
- *Furious that the coronavirus pandemic has wiped away any obvious corners for traditional comfort and consolation*
- *Angry that I've had to spend hours and days fighting for a legally due pension?*

Although some people comment about how well-balanced I appear, that's misleading. I still sometimes find myself in the morning shower crying, remembering the showers Herb and I shared before his stroke

awaiting the day when I decide whether to set up another guest room with new bedroom furniture or just keep the door shut. Right now, the room is filled with echoes.

in 2001. Even with all the responsibilities I'd assumed over these two decades, I *knew* we were together and felt imbued with the energy and strength to handle increasing responsibilities. Without him my persona is gone, along with my inherent sense of security. Special holidays and events are particularly difficult to face alone.

Now What?

Now I do ponder the questions others ask. *How am I?* Does the questioner really want to know? Or is it a proforma, empty way to demonstrate caring? This person may mean no harm and is just trying to empathize. But the contradiction is watching others try so hard to avoid thrusting themselves into an awkward situation that they so obviously do. To help well-meaning friends along, especially for those willing to bite the bullet and communicate, I sometimes suggest they rephrase and just ask me how I am on *that day*, explaining that each day is different-- some are up, some down, some memorable, some not. That helps one neighbor in particular feel more comfortable. Now each time I see Ramona she pauses, then asks "How are you *today*?" We both laugh.

Tears came at different times, often surprising me with the ferocity of feelings. I prefer to be alone during these times. There is no way anyone else can make things better so why encumber them with my fears and reactions? At least these quarantines have allowed me space to grieve quietly behind the mandated six feet of separation. Rena, a college friend living in Miami and a widow of 10 years' duration, explains that even with the passage of time, the pain of separation still lingers.

The Efforts of Others

Food is the last thing I wanted after Herb died or even now. Although I appreciate the continued thoughtfulness that comes in the form of cakes, cookies, chocolates, and even dinners sent to me, I'm not much of an eater. Under stress I revert to lockjaw. But I recognize that friends and neighbors want to reach out and share sweetness with me. Most contributions remain in the freezer because I do so little entertaining. Sometimes, when returning dishes and platters, I revert to an old-world custom and fill their returned dishes with shared pastries from others while they are fresh.

Even grieving presents special opportunities for humor. On the Sunday after Steve left, and I was at very low point, the doorbell rang. Standing there was a man holding a large brown bag by the bottom who urged me to take it from him the same way. Inside the bag were two one-gallon bottles of vodka with packages of chocolates wrapped around the necks of each bottle. These gifts came from Rena. Over the last two or three years, while I was caring for Herb, she'd quarterly mail me 30 pounds of chocolate kisses. Responding to my recent comment that the milk chocolate wasn't helping, Rena ratcheted up her powerful support. The vodka helped. But I've made it a point to drink only when sharing with Steve or my friend, Michael. The chocolates I continue to munch on my own. And often.

My Future Plans

How do I, after only a few months as a widow even know what my future plans will be? Why do people with so little imagination feel that they must go for the jugular with their questioning? I have no idea what I'm going to do now nor do I feel compelled to make any future plans at this time. I'm comfortable in my own home. Herb is all around me and that brings me comfort. Besides, I'm just a small cog. People are dying in major clusters around this country and the world from Covid-19. Few are traveling. I really have no place to go right now so why push it?

A couple of years ago I promised myself I would jump on a freighter after Herb died. Little did I know then that planes and ships around the world would be in lockdown because of because of this pandemic.

More recently I turned down an invitation from son Steve to join him in Istanbul, Turkey where he was traveling. With my passport current, this seemed like an exciting jaunt for a week or two, and certainly one that would break up the cluster of spider webs in my brain. Taking his suggestion seriously I checked into both the U.S. State Department and the Turkish Embassy to see whether because of the status of Covid-19 I would be permitted to return. Then I had second thoughts, recognizing that I was neither a great fan of the current Turkish government nor of the 15-20 hour-flight each way. Istanbul lost its great attractiveness and immediacy.

More Questions

Another question I've fielded too often: ***Do you have the funds to remain in your home?*** Now that question is both intrusive and objectionable. Unless the person doing the questioning has every intention to assume my mortgage or financial debt, why would they even ask it? I learned years ago to never question others about finances, debt or sex, but that doesn't deter these questioners with "good" intentions. And why is it assumed that widows and widowers must move to be near their children? Perhaps that's the reason why so many seniors are dying now in assisted living and nursing homes: because they've been placed there by their overly pressured families unable to absorb the responsibilities for their move. Children have their own lives and it's up to us, their parents, when physically and financially possible, to take care of ourselves and make our own decisions.

Herb and I prepared for these senior years and our independence. We were fortunate to cap our careers by working together in our own successful business for the almost 15 years before Herb's stroke. I remain open with my children about finances, estate, and their eventual inheritance. My children and grandchildren fortunately have their own lives, earn their own livings, and their right to independence, both personally and financially—as I do mine.

What Can Others Ask?

For starters, how about:
- *How are you today?*
- *Would you like some company?*
- *Want to join us for a Zoom conference?*
- *Want to join us for dinner? Bridge? Or a walk?*
- *Anything I/we can pick up for you from the store?*
- *Need any chores done that we can help with?*
- *Want some company?*

None of these are rocket science-conceived. Nor are they intrusive. But they are a welcome start.

Silver Singles

Bored through the teeth after just the first three months of my husband's passing, I googled a match-up service, *Silver Singles* that I saw advertised on TV. It claims to target a senior audience. I debated how friends and family might view my efforts so early into the mourning process but I also recognize that I can be dangerous when I am lonely. Shamefacedly flying "under the net," I filled out their SS application on line, declaring to myself my intention to do just research for this book. I was also curious to see who in my age range might also be stumbling around much like I am. But I really did not choose to meet anyone locally. Distance during Covid-19 offered a safety.

Entry questions were actually helpful and caused me to examine myself post-Herb. In particular, it made me think about what I was really bringing to this new phase of my life and interests. I answered the questions truthfully, even listing my true age, but otherwise chose to remain behind a barrier with only a college nickname and a secondary, non-identifying email address.

Considering it an investment in amusement and forced "social networking" I bit the bullet and made the initial investment of $106 (including sales tax) for a three-month membership. I shared my one available photo, an old "author" photo, and the only one still filed on my computer.

I chose Silver Singles rather than J-Date because I prefer local anonymity. I filled out my "personality" description, chose a "safe" mileage radius of 300 miles, assuming that distance wouldn't really make much difference during this pandemic because no one was traveling. I certainly did not want visitors. This effort became more of an amusement than need.

Social Networking

Responders came in a flood, often three a day for almost those three months. Most were obviously retired and in the age range of 79-89, with the majority at the upper limits of this age range. Each supposedly brought at least a Bachelor's degree. Even more declared they had masters and doctorates. Although I'd specified a wide radius, the majority fell even further afield geographically from my request, reaching from Chicago and Charlotte, VA, to Baltimore and New York. And where I'd specified my religious affiliation as Jewish, most listed themselves as Christian and predominately Catholic. One was agnostic, three Jewish, and one Muslim. In general, the widowers reported they were "good listeners", enjoyed reading and television, and did some gardening. Their quest for passion and companionship ranked high. Most stated upfront that they preferred to share expenses.

There were two specific contacts who stood out because they seemed more active and venturesome. The first, even more energetic than the others, listed himself as a former Navy and commercial pilot, loved travel, and was currently taking courses in law school. I was moved to respond but did so cautiously. I declared three provisos up front:

- *That he not be divorced*
- *Be currently in good health, and*
- *Not be a Trump supporter.*

All three of these criteria are important to me. And to my values. But obviously I struck a nerve.

By the next day, this gentleman had totally expunged his entire *Silver Singles'* account and disappeared. *Silver Singles* continued to send daily "applicants" but without my response they began tapering down. Still, the most eager respondents were aged from 85-89. Some obviously were photographed as "selfies", sitting directly in front of their computers, not very flattering.

A Second Try

There was another candidate, toward the tail end, who, from his photo and description actually looked alive and active. I messaged him through **Silver Singles** and we seemed to go back and forth for a couple of messages. He said that he held a doctorate in business management and owned a heavy equipment construction business in northern Virginia that he was in the process of selling. After the third message he suggested that we email or phone directly. I sent him an email address that did not list my name but then he disappeared without follow-up.

Stunned by this response I contacted SS to see why such an action might occur. Their spokesman cautioned me that sometimes their system is used by those intent on committing fraud by targeting single senior women. The spokesman asked whether this man had tried to contact me directly. Sure enough, one week later the following email message appeared:

Hello Bee18,

I am scott. I got your email from silver singles. How are you doing? Write back if you received this email.

Now clued into the obvious dangers, my immediate response was:

Scott, I think you're going to have to prove your existence and legitimacy this time around. Have already talked with Silver Singles about how and why you would withdraw your information and have been warned about people like you. Back off.

I did not expect to hear back and have since cancelled Silver Singles and moved on. I may reconsider in future months and try again.

What made Silver Singles head and shoulders above other groups I briefly dabbled with, like Match, is that they include specific information about widowhood or divorce status, religion, and education. Others don't. Obviously you have no way to affirm any of the information. The different responses over several months were distracting during a difficult period of loneliness, loss and boredom. I enjoyed looking through daily emails and could relate to others wandering through their own searches for companionship and life fulfillment, each hoping not to end this latter segment of their lives alone. But these two experiences have underscored for me that open experiences can be dangerous and that any personal information must be limited. There are too many

---

18   An old college nickname made by putting my three initials together.

stories about adventurers who provide false IDs and take advantage of lonely widows.

Not A Promising Investment

My intention in looking into a matchmaking service was, through curiosity, to monitor those who might choose to be matched with me. It's been a beneficial exercise which, I must admit, has added warmth and humor to isolated mornings on the computer. Finding a match is obviously tempting. So many of us are searching for companionship, especially those who have experienced prior relationships and would prefer to open a new chapter for life and living. Perhaps if I ever do this again, as so many of my single friends reluctantly admit they have and continue to do, I might specify a younger male audience by at least five or ten years.

I don't in any way downgrade these gentlemen who have taken the time to read and respond to my bio. It takes courage to open oneself up to chance. Numbers of them must have also had wonderful relationships, families, lifetime careers, and are now as lonely as I am. I hope they each find a new companion who will share their pursuits and help them feel whole again.

In all sincerity, an older male companion leading to reactivating my caregiver role is not at all enticing to me. I recognize that my primary challenge at this stage of life is to figure out who I am *now* and what I want for myself. I didn't before, nor do I now, need to find that gigolo that I'd earlier joked about. But admittedly, this whole process was certainly distracting.

Reflections

It took years of wandering, a broken engagement and a few in-between relationships to find that special person I was seeking to together forge a good life. I never sought to have someone "take care of me." Life between two competitive spirits wasn't perfect but Herb and I learned to merge our talents and our relationship and build something far stronger than either of us expected.

One of the strongest commonalities my husband and I shared was the love of life-long education. We each completed our advanced degrees after we were married. Herb's doctorate was in business and economics and mine as a masters in history. Throughout our marriage, and, even after Herb's stroke, we continued to take courses, separately and together at area colleges and through special programs. It was critical to us and our marriage that we share ideas, accomplishments and even leadership. After Herb's stroke, my physical challenge was to toss the wheelchair into the trunk during all seasons and find imaginative ways to continue our high quality of life. The rewards and sparks we gained from learning and sharing made our mutual effort far more meaningful. I have not experienced that same interest or intellect from any of the responses I've so far had. But there always remains a remote possibility.

Lessons Learned

1. *You are not compelled to answer ridiculous or thoughtless questions.*
2. *Keep open the lines of communication.* Try to turn them around so that friends become helpful and you find companionship.
3. *Widowhood is a time for self-reflection and accounting* for who you, as an individual, are *now.*
4. *Assess your financial and personal needs.* This is the time to take inventory.
5. *Do not feel compelled to make any major decisions* unless you absolutely have to because of finances.
6. *Find pursuits and interests that tap into your curiosity and imagination.*
7. *Yes, you can join whatever groups interest you,* including matchmaking programs, but be wary of any commitments at this early time. And be especially cautious about disclosing *any* personal information until you have Googled or otherwise verified that person's name and reputation. In case of any question, you can also obtain arrest records on line for a small sum, which is certainly worthwhile. Be aware that not all these people use their own names. I would go so far, if there is a next

time, to more fully check out anyone through any of these extra means.

8. *A healthy sense of curiosity means that you are alive.*
9. *You are the only one to "save yourself".*
10. *Feel confident that you can row your own boat* and make your own decisions.

CHAPTER X

ATTACK OF THE ALIENS

Some of the saddest stories I continue to hear from widowed friends are about sudden family grabs for their estate by children, step children, former spouses, and multi-generational relatives who consider wills and estates ripe for plucking. Death and estates form tricky personal issues that are open to a great level of complexity, especially when names are purposefully excluded from the wills. My friends refer to these interlopers as the "aliens," absent until the scent of money beckons.

The Unexpected

Some whom I've interviewed have reactions to being unexpectedly overwhelmed by sloppy family business partnerships and divisions of properties, as well as unfamiliar stock and tax liabilities. Fighting these onslaughts often requires additional expenses for lawyers and invites the higher authority (and cost) of probate judges who step in.

Challenges come not only from past spousal relationships but also from immediate family members and result in family divisions. A friend shared with me an aggressive act by one of her four children who questioned her late father's will, feeling that she'd been "cheated" by an unequal apportionment. Apparently, because this daughter was wealthier, the parent had unevenly divided his estate. The daughter took matters into her own hand and insisted that her own daughter, the granddaughter, break into her dead grandfather's computer to prove her case. Acting under this direction, the granddaughter copied and removed designated pages from both will and business papers. She even changed his password. It required civil action and ripples of criminal action and mistrust that have since severed the family relationship.

Family Minefields

I am not an attorney because I never made it all the way through law school. I simply pass along information that I have gleaned in studying this subject. And for the record, I assume no responsibility. My bottom line is to advise you to hire a really good estate attorney, well-schooled in this particular legal specialty. One way or another, when you expect to fight off an alien threat, you should prepare yourself well before the bereavement.

Minefields abound in families. Widows and widowers sitting on comfortable estates often become targets for biological heirs who have difficulty managing their own money and believe they deserve a larger share than their more comfortable and conservative siblings. Prevailing on the surviving parent to "share" more "based on need" not only puts the remaining parent's estate in jeopardy but also opens the way to resentment by other siblings who have their own needs and expect to be equally included in the full mix.

Parents are torn by this dissension among their children. Often children who have been more conservative in their money management skills resent those more profligate who are rewarded with extra. They assume with unequal distribution, therefore, that they are less loved by the surviving parent. During this contest, say my friends, children can easily brush aside the collective investment parents have already made in their college educations and weddings and other "bailouts". This tug of war can threaten the surviving parent's remaining cashable balance and home.

Children from an Earlier Marriage

Another attack looms suddenly from the children of an earlier marriage. This can involve those who may have been out of communication for 20 or 30 years, and have perhaps rejected all contact, including when the biological parent was dying. These "aliens" believe they have every right to attack the settlement of any estate that does not include them. "You owe me," seems to be their major cudgel.

MaryJo, another dear friend, recently shared with me the attack by her partner's daughters a few years ago while he was still taking care of his mentally and physically impaired wife, their mother. He was regularly providing meds, food, cleaning, and personal care even though he had already moved out. Jim's two grown daughters conspired to relieve him not only of his wife's care but also his entire estate. They hired an attorney who filed divorce papers and charged neglect of their mother, already in the mid-stages of dementia. The court awarded the divorce and appointed a guardian and caregiver who assumed the same responsibilities that Jim had handled over the previous five years without any fanfare. Within one month this caregiver placed his wife, their mother, in a nursing home with expenses that wiped out both Jim and the estate financially. When the greedy daughters requested control along with a divvy of the remaining estate, the court informed them that all residual monies had been repaid to the state and county for their mother's care. In this case, no one won.

So much of this contest over estate brings heartache and vulnerability to the bereaved survivor, not to mention the additional time and cost to hire an executor or attorney to examine the original will and defend against associated technicalities and charges. Sometimes even witnesses who may have attested to the wills decades ago are recalled, assuming they are still alive. This tug of war involves additional time and emotional impact to their attack.

The Disinherited

To be more explicit, let us assume a spouse left a last will and testament that was properly signed and witnessed. [19] In most states the surviving spouse and direct descendants inherit first according to the will.

Where it gets complicated is if the decedent is survived by several children and one, for whatever reason, is excluded from this will. The outlier child may have to prove that he/she has legal standing to establish that the subsequent will is invalid for some reason. Complications extend from whether this excluded child was named in an earlier will; is named but receives a less substantial inheritance than siblings/half siblings; or is completely disinherited. The first challenge is to establish whether this eliminated child has legal standing to contest the will. And second, whether he/she has cause to establish that the deceased parent

---

19   Again, I can only suggest but do not have legal standing to discuss the repercussions for those who die without a will, otherwise known as "intestate succession".

was under duress, or was mentally incapacitated, when signing the more recent will and testament. Their goal is obviously to invalidate the subsequent will for whatever reason.

Joyce recently told me about a very wealthy friend of hers, a childless widow, who intended to remove her husband's cousin from her will for a host of good reasons. She had her attorney draw up a new will but did not have time to sign it before her unexpected death. This cousin, her closest living relative, benefited from the entire inheritance.

Important to remember is that those engaged in fighting current provisions, even assuming the court's verdict goes against them, have little to lose by challenging the will other than attorney's fees. Many consider this to be a valid investment in their future riches.

Contests over wills and estates represent a complex area of estate law. A will can outline an individual's intended beneficiaries, identify the assets they own, and specify how those assets will be distributed after the spouse passes away.

Before bereavement, it is the responsibility of both spouses to consult with an attorney who specializes in this type of probate law to ensure they have legal standing to update and defend against any overturn of their joint wills. It's also vital that you choose an attorney who will remain in practice for many subsequent years to hopefully protect against potential challenges.

Lessons Learned

1. *In remarrying, be sure that you have established either a pre-nuptial agreement* or drawn up an iron clad, marital property agreement with a new will, especially should you have large assets that you do <u>not</u> want to pass directly to a current or previous spouse.

2. *Be aware that marriage to a new partner may impact the inheritance of children* from a previous relationship on either side.

3. *Create or update an existing estate plan when planning to remarry* that reflects your children's interests and wishes.

4. *Consider giving your children from a first marriage a direct gift* through a Last Will and Testament or establishment of a trust as a way to protect their interests.

5. *Each spouse should specify through the will all financial designations* to charities, non-profits, non-immediate family members, and friends.

6. *Before considering remarriage, create an estate plan* and update an existing one to identify your assets, designate beneficiaries and joint owners, your executors, and also specify how you want your assets to be passed to your spouse and children, both natural and step.

7. *Consider whether to even choose remarriage with its legal complications.* Many people today find it convenient and less threatening to simply live together.

8. *Choose an astute attorney well established in estate law* to set up both wills for a second marriage--and preferably one not likely to retire within the next 5 to 10 years should there be a later contesting issue.

9. *Be knowledgeable about your spouse's finances* and comfortable about how the new will includes your wishes and protects your assets. Keep all legal agreements updated and readily available to both spouses.

10. *Do not trust to "good faith" or verbal agreements.* Require special protections for family issues and partnerships and *treat all children the same or be prepared for blowback.* Leaving more to one child or leaving one out entirely is asking for anger and challenges later. Also keep in mind that stepchildren aren't automatically treated as children for legal purposes. To share in inheritance, they must be specifically named. *Your documentation may also need revisions* if you move from one state to another.

CHAPTER XI

REGRET VS. GUILT

I've been told that guilt is rather common in death. I didn't feel guilt after Herb died because I knew I'd done everything in my power to care for him for this almost one-third of our marriage, which is why I almost left this discussion out of my coverage.

Yes, I regretted then and even now that I hadn't given Herb more morphine to make the end of his life faster and gentler. No question about that. But Herb knew that I loved him with all my heart and still do because I told him that again and again. Underscoring my promise to take care of him I kept my pledge that he would have a rich quality of life based on all I could do. Over these two decades, I'd argued with the physicians, traveled from one system to another seeking better answers and treatments, doled out medications, adapted to unfamiliar systems and equipment, learned to do the bed exercises, insert catheters and hearing aids, and like a master sergeant transferred him from one chair to another when he could no longer move by himself. Walking him up and down the garage ramp, I also learned to pray. Hard, especially when he stopped in the middle and could go no further.[20]

Divine Intervention

Each time we got into trouble, often in the center of that ramp where there was no turning back, I prayed directly to G-d asking for divine power to help us make it up the next ten feet, followed by that one last high step into the back foyer of the house. Sometimes, most times, we made it—followed by another prayer of thanks. Sometimes we didn't.

---

20   I am going to confess here about those times when I did feel intervention by a higher power, especially walking halfway up that garage ramp when Herb could suddenly go no further. With the cell phone and wheelchair resting in the trunk of the car, we somehow with prayer made it up the full ramp, over the back step, through the foyer and onto the living room recliner. There is no other way to acknowledge the impossible. I know I couldn't have done it myself.

I tried my best then to gently settle Herb down so that I could call the Shaker Heights EMS and ask for their help. These good people got to know us and even kept a copy of our book, ONE STROKE, TWO SURVIVORS in their library.

When Herb felt he no longer could walk the ramp, I set down another portable ramp covering that top step, transferred him from the car to his wheelchair, and pushed him in the chair up the double ramp. It was a heavy weight for me that eventually caused an inguinal hernia. But that extra effort bought us more time to get out of the house and remain independent.

Never a Saint

I must admit I did feel some guilt at a mid-point into the stroke when I was getting Herb washed and ready for bed. In a bad mood, he scowled while seated in his wheelchair at the bathroom sink, and then smacked my arm hard resisting the sponge bath. Angry and tired, I picked up the small basin of warm water that was positioned in the sink in front of us and poured it over his head. We both were shocked! And for a moment, just a moment, it actually felt good to react after keeping my frustration so welled up. But shock certainly cooled off that heated moment when I had to dry and change him from top to bottom. When Herb was comfortably in bed, I finished washing the floor and walls. This was not something I did again. Nor did he.

Life was trying for both of us and there were often difficult moments. Dr. Elizabeth Dreben, the rehab psychologist whom we shared, was the specialist who really helped both of us to work out our conflicting emotions. I requested her support early in Herb's rehab program at MetroHealth Hospital in 2001. We continued to see her every three weeks for the full duration of Herb's post stroke journey.[21] She helped us, especially me, to talk out conflicting emotions and frustration. Herb was less communicative than I but he listened, understood my frustration and fatigue, and tried his best to cooperate. Several of Dr. Dreben's best suggestions were that I not consider myself as martyr and indeed spend the money to bring on more caregivers for longer breaks.

21   Dr. Dreben visited us at home several times when Herb could no longer move out of the house and brought holiday Purim cookies she'd baked. As Herb would say, it was a special relationship.

At the beginning of stroke recovery, I was resentful because I felt Herb had gotten us into this position and changed both our lives by being so lax about his own healthcare. In ONE STROKE, I wrote an entire chapter about anger. We knew also that life brings both the good and the bad, sickness and health. But knowing and accepting are sometimes miles apart, especially on the receiving end. And through this counseling Herb recognized that, in spite of my grumbling, I stood beside him all the way. I even wrote a poem about us:

Though You May Stumble

Though you may stumble
I'll be right there beside you
To catch you
Rebalance you
Protect you.

Though you may forget
I'll be right there beside you
To remind you
Laugh with you
Reassure you.

Though you may grow tired
I'll be right there beside you
To encourage you
Stimulate you
Love you.

No, I was not a saint. Far from it. But I tried with all my heart to make life better for Herb and to let him know he was still a man in my eyes; and that the stroke did not diminish his personhood nor my love for him. Knowing we had only a little more time, I continued to remind Herb of how much he meant to me. Throughout Herb's bedridden time I often climbed into his hospital bed with him and we cuddled and talked. In the last days and even minutes, I was back in the bed (I usually closed the bedroom door to the 24/7 team and turned off the monitor). Herb had no words by then but I reminded him of the trips we'd taken, his accomplishments, how proud I was of him, and how deeply I loved him. His last words to me, only two days before he died, was "I love you." Those words will sustain me forever.

Other Views

My former roommate, Flossie, now in a nursing home, during a telephone conversation yelled at me. From her muddled memories[22], she accused me of forcing Herb years ago to attend theatre in Stratford and Niagara-on-the-Lake, Ontario. She blasted me, saying "You made him go!" I can assure you, dear reader, in almost 57 years of marriage, it was rare or nonexistent that I ever made my husband do anything he didn't want to do.

Margaret, a good friend, former boss, and also a new widow, recently wrote about her own feelings of regret. *"I keep thinking of things I should have done differently or just things I should have talked with John about, but I didn't. I didn't realize that it is a common thing for widows to attempt to cope. I thought it was only my issue but now am beginning to wonder about whether this isn't a common response."*

William shares another view. *"Guilt or regret! Is there a difference? I regret most of all that our souls, our hearts didn't talk to each other. I think of this every day, but am condemned never to know. I regret that I didn't appreciate her wonderful, human qualities as a wife and as a mother, constantly revisiting in my mind now the selfless and loving acts she did. I regret I didn't love her enough. I love her now more than anything in the world."*

My sister-in-law Lois, who lost my brother four years ago and is in 24/7 nursing care in her own home, disagrees, *"I don't feel a bit of guilt. I never did anything other than what Alan wanted. I did absolutely everything to make him comfortable...and I felt so blessed."*

---

22   I didn't realize in this last telephone call that she was now suffering from dementia. Sadly, it was the last time we ever talked to one another.

So, perhaps guilt really refers to unfinished hopes and aspirations that we, the survivors, may carry with us. I suspect much of this reaction may occur when there hasn't been sufficient time to talk and express our final goodbyes directly to our spouses.

Lessons Learned

1. *Ask for professional help.* Seeing a psychologist or social worker to work through lingering feelings of guilt or regrets can be very helpful. Bereavement groups can also help to work through these emotions about end-of-life challenges.

2. *Advance planning between you and your spouse about end-of-life decisions* is critical. With this planning you share responsibility and direction, minimizing any feelings of guilt on the part of the survivor.

3. *Remember the good stages of life* with a full heart.

4. *Comfort and support yourself by writing down beautiful thoughts* and memories in a journal of positive reflections, especially when memories begin to blur.

5. *Forgive yourself.* Instead of concentrating what you didn't do, focus on the good acts you did and what you most appreciated.

6. *When ready, let go* and move on.

CHAPTER XII

NEXT STEPS

The Quest

As a woman, with a graduate degree in history and life-long career in communications, it's my turn now to figure out what I'm going to do when I grow up. I've had lots of time during this Covid-19 virus-sequestering to think. And fortunately for me, I also have comfortable finances (assuming the world and stock market remain intact following the presidential-2020 campaign). My three children are very supportive and fortunately accept me as sole beneficiary. They already know that my estate will be divided into three equal parts after I have passed. But with Herb gone only months at the beginning of this writing, I must admit to pondering options for what I'm going to do next.

I decided to query others as I put together my own roadmap recognizing that this juncture is just one of a series of major passages in my life. In the late 1970s when I came out of a ten-year "hiatus" that included three children, a Master's degree, and a number of community leadership roles, few jobs were available for women with young children regardless of past work experience. The question most often tossed condescendingly at me was "Can you type?" *Yes*, I retorted as I turned my back and walked out of these offices, *but not for you!* I was frustrated at my lack of perceived value even though I carried a portfolio of work experience with titles from the largest public relations company in New York City.

After considerable research, including reading Gail Sheehy's PASSAGES I put together a program called ***"HOMEMAKER RE-ENTRY TO THE BUSINESS WORLD,"*** and targeted widows, divorcees', volunteers, and others who had never worked outside their homes. The concept was to help these women recognize and add value to their own job-hunting experiences. I convinced Columbus Technical Institute and Ohio University to provide sponsorship and then using my public relations skills filled all multi-sessions to capacity. Toward the conclusion of the program courses, I invited one of my panelists, the president of an advertising agency, to have lunch with me. Within a week, I went to work for her and, within a month, became her director of public relations. Margaret, whom I interviewed earlier, and I have remained good friends with throughout all these years. We continue to be mutually supportive through our bereavements.

A second turn at bat followed Herb's stroke. I was disappointed to find that of all the personal and clinical stroke books on the market, none answered pragmatic questions about how to use a commode or kick the medical doors open. Searching for these answers led to writing two books: **ONE STROKE, TWO SURVIVORS** and **LESSONS LEARNED: STROKE RECOVERY FROM A CAREGIVER'S PERSPECTIVE**. Both books were published by The Cleveland Clinic. These are the first and only books that cover both perspectives (in different fonts), of the stroke survivor and the caregiver.[23] Together Herb and I recognized a glaring need and answered questions that many in these two categories did not even know how to ask.

New Challenges

Now I'm again at a crossroads and must figure out who I am today and what it's going to take to keep me challenged and functioning into my future. Obviously, I'm not the only senior widow or widower raising this question. You are too or you wouldn't be reading this manuscript now.

With all of this in mind, I talked with my friends and friends of their friends about bereavement experiences. Among the questions I asked about this new phase of their lives:

- *What age were you when your spouse died and after how many years of marriage?*
- *How difficult was the paper-completion process and did you need outside support?*

---

23   ONE STROKE is still the only book on the market that presents stroke from both the caregiver's and the stroke survivor's perspectives, not always the same. Both books are available on the Internet for free download.

- *How supportive were friends and family during and following the initial few months?*
- *Who among your friends provided the most beneficial support and why?*
- *How has life changed for you?*
- *When did you resume some level of emotional stability; how and why?*

Bill's Campaign

Bill, aged 90, following four years of widowhood and encouragement from his family, sold his home in Queens, NY, and moved to Atlanta from New York City to live independently near his older son. He chose an all-adult facility and began a major effort to find a companionable woman.

Bill approached several women in his new apartment house whom he targeted one at a time. He wrote poetry, sent roses, talked up a storm. But nothing happened until he decided that, in his heart of hearts, he really wanted even more was to resurrect his love of the lindy swing dance. He emailed a photo that showed him dancing in a roadhouse out on the floor, surrounded by at least 10 young women who circled him in a cloud of enthusiasm. Bill returned the second week and then the third, each time drawing an even larger group.

That first photo taken by his son—of him cutting a rug with the ladies surrounding him and cheering--was inspiring. Some weeks later, friends introduced Bill to a widow of similar background who also loved swing dancing. They make quite a number now and are happily living together. Bill has also joined Toastmaster's Club, a feat I'd been encouraging him to make years ago.

Today Helen cheers him on each time he makes a Zoom-Toastmaster's presentation. I enjoy watching on-line the enthusiasm on his face as well as hers. Life is now pretty exciting for Bill who is rediscovering himself and has found a new zest for life. Although Covid-19 has cramped immediate dancing aspirations, Bill and Helen continue to take long walks and enjoy life together.

Discovering Individuality

Another friend, Tena, became a widow ten years ago following her husband's long illness. Well educated with a doctorate, she worked until her own retirement and has found joy in her independence today by doing exactly what she feels like doing when she feels like doing it. She remains in her home, travels (at least she did before the pandemic) to visit her children and grandchildren on both coasts, has learned how to use Zoom and other programs, hooks rugs, knits, reads, and loves her freedom and individuality. With no one else to cater to Tena enjoys her own personhood. Tena found strength and support through her synagogue, before the pandemic, to identify a community of like-minded people who invited her to join them for the Mourners' Kaddish service, shared twice daily for those in bereavement. She left after the period of mourning but returned some years later because there is no time limitation and feels very comfortable in the daily evening section that is now broadcast on Zoom.

Tena's advice to new widows and widowers: *"Everybody has a different time period for mourning. People react differently. I needed to become a part of something, a group that welcomed me, so I could connect with others. My synagogue group provided a comfortable reentry."*

Taking the Time to Process

I've remained friends with a former roommate, Rae, who, by coincidence, was married on the same day and same year as Herb and I. Rae's husband Manny died five years ago on that cruise that I mentioned earlier. She explains that she took time to process not only Manny's sudden death but also the paper work and functions that overwhelmed her. When others questioned how long she was going to remain in her home of 50 years, she responded, *"This isn't a speed contest. I haven't disposed of everything, even today, and have taken my time because I could. My husband enjoyed professional business clothing so I sent his suits to people looking for jobs. I'm still in a selection process for what I need and have to do and what can wait a little longer. I have a lot of support and am grateful for those wonderful years with my husband."*

Finding a New Mate

Another friend who also goes back to our single days in Baltimore lost her husband about four years ago. Much as she loved him, Judie knew from the beginning that single life was not for her. *"I missed the closeness of being a pair, of caring for someone and being cared for in return."* She didn't shirk the grieving process but even with close female friends, and a snuggly, little dog, she found that constant loneliness was too much to bear. Recognition and introductions came through friends who along with her son introduced her to the father of one of his medical partners.

Judie and Sheldon met over a phone call he had placed following the battery of recommendations targeted at him. Judy recounted, *"Geographically situated in different parts of the country, we spoke for over an hour in the first call, followed by once a day that turned into multiple times each day for several months until we met in person. We both felt the physical chemistry. This has been a wonderful relationship. But I still love and miss my husband as does Sheldon for his late wife. We sometimes joke that our two spouses must have together formed this match for us."*

A Matching Story

Sheldon lost his wife only a few months before Judie lost her husband. He also discovered the loneliness of being single. Male friends whose company he had enjoyed before as part of couple's get togethers became remote. *"We really had nothing to say to each other."*

Sheldon, married for 61 years, had little advance warning. *"My wife, aged 87, was always the healthy one...until stage 4 pancreatic cancer suddenly reared its head and she went within three and a half months. For the next month or so friends gathered around... and then they and my children returned to their own lives."* He joined a bereavement group *"but the 10-12 participants were as emotionally wiped out as I was. You can get through the days, even the meals. But when night comes, you're all alone and life is terrible."*

Today Judie and Sheldon share her home in Florida during the winter, and his home, outside of Boston, in the cooler summer months. They don't intend to marry. And they don't have to. But they have become close and fully enjoy one another's company. *"Going alone is no picnic. But when you have somebody to talk to and share with, life is good for both of us."*

What Do Others Say?

Phyllis sums up her situation succinctly by recounting *"I have learned to focus on gratitude, which works for me."*

Cindy describes her current situation as *"Remaining in touch with friends is crucial to your attitude and sense of balance."* She met her husband in college and they married immediately after graduation. She followed her life as mother and homemaker (not to exclude two graduate degrees and teaching for many years) with a successful career as editor of a major local publication. Prior to the coronavirus, Cindy found community with other widows, some from her previous social group, often by organizing dinner and theatre nights. Now she remains active as a playwright leading weekly Zoom sessions with Stagewrights, a playwriting group attached to the Ensemble Theatre, in Cleveland Heights, Ohio, as well as through afternoon get-togethers with friends, one at a time.

My Way: High Tea

In recent months, particularly the colder ones, I watched as Covid-19 has isolated many of the widows and widowers I know. Most are fearful of their vulnerability and health issues as seniors but high tea on the patio did serve as a non-threatening way to socialize. People were absolutely free to do as they please, and to choose what was most comfortable for them. Often these invitations became reciprocal and offered a wonderful opportunity to get out and socialize even with masks. Isolation will continue through winter months and hopefully when warm weather returns we can once again resume our gatherings outdoors.

So, Who Am I?

I am still trying to figure that out, especially since I do not find age particularly restricting. And I prefer not to dwell on it.

Hibernation until Covid-19 runs its course is not for me or my temperament. Admittedly, I am a news junky, especially as I became engulfed in the 2020 presidential election. I have lots of energy, am a night and long-distance driver, and yearn for the great gates to really open wide so I can be on my way. Nor am I overweight, even with all the milk chocolate I munch on daily. And I don't intend to turn gray unless my hairdresser decides to lock her doors again in another enforced pandemic.

I remember hearing stories about my father who set the example. At the same age he used to chauffeur other seniors in his small village for shopping or special excursions. He and my stepmother would even drive nine hours each way with no stopping overnight, from Ellenville, NY to Cleveland, at least once or twice a year to visit us.

I enjoy hiking, travel, theatre, dancing, mingling, socializing, writing plays and books—and especially hugging--if only these opportunities were available. Oh, how I miss hugging! Perhaps that will return someday, if only I can wait patiently until the Covid-19 storm passes and the Munchkins come out to play again.

And since mid-October I have taken ownership/guardianship of a little Corgi puppy, now six months old, whom I've named "Winnie". Once again I'm involved in house-breaking, walking and the parenting process. And that doesn't even include the reconciliation process, attempting to resolve problems between Loganberry and his new brother, not an easy match. No longer can I sleep late because I'm up taking the pup out by 4:30 a.m. So *"once more into the breech"* go I.

Future planning includes tentative 2021 thoughts about travel on the Trans-Siberian Railway all the way to Mongolia. A friend of my son Steve's has asked us to return the ashes of a friend to a family in Ulan Ude[24] and assures me that Steve and I will be welcomed as their guests were we to take this trip. I've long read about Siberia, its beauty in the summers (assuming that the 90+ degree temperatures in 2020 are an aberration and do not become "typical"). I am eager for

---

24   On the border between Siberia and Mongolia.

adventure but would have to establish certain preconditions: including that I have choices of low carbohydrate foods and can both dental floss and sleep comfortably on a pillow at night. And, of course, would have to have a dear friend move into my home to take care of Winnie and Loganberry for the two weeks while I take this trip. Who knows realistically whether this new Covid-19 vaccine will work, let alone be effective. But I still need to dream.

Reflections

When I was just entering my 80s, still with Herb, I reflected on this new stage of life and wrote what may someday may become my own eulogy.

Reflections on Turning 80

Why is it that we never really expect to grow old? Older yes but old seems too far down the pike to really have significance. If fortunate, we've watched our parents and teachers age. We've seen old movies and googled the same actors and actresses in their current ages to witness the multiple levels of debris that come with the years. Some still look really good. Others show the harshness of life and living, the unhappiness, and even the anger.

Yes, there are those who retain a sparkle, life-flaming eyes, wrinkles set by actual not faked smiles, and the sense of purpose and accomplishments that score a life well lived. These are the men and women I so admire.

But what really is accomplishment? What do we hope to leave behind as our legacy when it's our turn to go? Is it the trust fund we leave for our children and grandchildren? Are we judged by a long marriage? Our children's accomplishments? Is it what we say about ourselves or, better yet, what others say about us? Does it all boil down to a eulogy that we ourselves are denied hearing? Or can our memory be as simple as a touch, a smile, a special word of thanks?

As adults, wives, husbands, mothers, in-laws, friends, neighbors, co-workers, co-religionists, shoppers, professionals, non-professionals we each represent many facets that others, including even ourselves, may not recognize or value.

In the final analysis, perhaps it's really up to us to record our own eulogies about how we want to be remembered, what we aspired to--even when we didn't fulfil our best intentions. Who better than we ourselves can attest to how close we came to achieving our most cherished goals?

Berenice E. Kleiman, 10-22-17

SO?

Who knows what 2021 and subsequent years will bring, especially when combined with all three legs of this current stool: pandemic, economic recession, and unsettled political situation in the U.S.? But, for now, it's really nice to fall asleep with a dream. And an ambitious Russian travel agent, who picked me up the internet, is already planning this Siberian trip.

Yes, Herb is gone and I am alone. But I know as I look out at this last segment of my life that I don't have to be lonely. I have friends and family. And, maybe someday, I'll find a new companion. That step is too soon to even contemplate. Right now, it's up to me to find purpose in my own life.

In the meantime, I hope my words and thoughts will help others take their own next step into the future. Through this book I hope to leave a trail of little white pebbles for other widows and widowers to follow. That would certainly give meaning to this exercise that has preoccupied and even distracted me for these early months.

Lessons Learned

1. **People react to loss differently** and there's no need to limit your personal period for mourning.

2. ***Try to become part of something outside yourself*** so that you can connect with others as comfortably as possible.

3. ***Accept any and all invitations*** (especially when Covid-19 clears.) An unwritten rule of widowhood is that these friends probably won't make that offer again if you decline.[25]

4. ***Aging is a challenge:*** without becoming morose, work as hard as you can to remain as mentally and physically sharp as possible.

5. ***When you feel overwhelmed and off balance***, remember you have to take only one step at a time.

6. ***Your ability to survive depends on you***, your attitude, and your independence.

7. ***Find some way you can reach out and help others.***

8. ***Find an idea that excites you***, one that you may long have thought of doing but put off.

9. ***Consider doing something special or spontaneous each day***, even if it's just watching a little chipmunk, a flower, taking a photograph or writing a letter.

10. ***Reread some of the beautiful letters and cards you've received*** and take the time to recognize how you, yourself, are appreciated.

---

25   And they may not make it again even if you accept. Also be especially mindful to pay your own way. This is a huge part of your independence (and perhaps even subsequent invitations.)

CHAPTER XIII

EPILOGUE

Currently, at six months into widowhood, and involved in another frosty Cleveland winter, I am finishing the writing of this book and I have a six-month old puppy sleeping under my computer desk. Who thought I would take on this responsibility at my age, but why not? Here is a little boy who loves, trusts, demands and even pulls me on ice in his quest for squirrels.[26] Most friends seem to think I'm a little crazy.

But, as A. E. Houseman wrote:

The laws of God, the laws of man,
He may keep that will and can;
Not I: let God and man decree
Laws for themselves and not for me;
And if my ways are not as theirs
Let them mind their own affairs....

How could I not restart with little Winnie? A litter of pups was born around my block in mid-July and in early October 2020 I became the mother to Winnie, a handsome Pembroke Welsh Corgi. Not an easy step this adoption because he teethes on everything, especially my shoes and furniture. And since he's not fully housebroken, requires walking early a.m. as my attempt to keep his cage dry. Much like when my children were infants, I now move around during the daytime badly in need of a couple of extra hours of sleep.

---

26   Yes, I am searching for a dog trainer. I can handle the basics of "sit", "down", "come" but am beyond my capabilities to teach him to "heel", the most basic command of all. I am discovering that dog trainers are a highly professional and well-paid service category. Some packages they offer may even be equivalent to tuition for a first year of college. Perhaps that gigolo might prove less expensive when all the training and vet expenses are tallied.

Much to his breed's description, he is tenacious, bold, outgoing, playful, friendly, protective and very loving. But since he realistically needs at least one real live boy to fill his life and absorb his playfulness, I've hired my teenage neighbor to hopefully run the pup ragged for an afternoon half hour after his Covid-home studies. Otherwise, "I'm on" for the walks every hour on the hour as well as the training. And for the "accidents" around the house I'm sure Herb is looking down laughing at me and saying "Be careful of what you wish for."

But when I consider the options,, I think I'm way ahead. My cat Loganberry obviously disagrees and has taken exclusive refuge upstairs on my bed and away from this intruder. Perhaps someday we can effect a reconciliation. Perhaps.

In the meantime, I've joined the dog walkers I used to envy from my bedroom window early in the morning and evening as they promenaded along their regular routes. While I may have some regrets as the nights turn longer and colder, I must admit that walking Winnie late at night or in the early morning in my backyard, offers some blissful advantages, including calm. I am relearning star formations. And nothing is as welcoming as the wagging of Winnie's tail when he sees me for the first time in the early morning as I approach his pen. Even with the plastic newspaper bags hanging out of my pocket, positioned

next to a bag of puppy treats, I don't regret the responsibility to "pick up" his droppings. I reward his gifts with praise and a couple of treats.

And just maybe, maybe, little Winnie will begin to fill some of the mound of emptiness that yawns in my heart. At least he makes me laugh. And the days now don't seem as long as they've previously been.

THE END

NEXT STEP NOTES

ACKNOWLEDGEMENTS

I'm deeply indebted to the friends who have read early versions of this book and challenged me to make it a better one: Dr. Tena Rosner, Dr. Manjula Shah, Rena Ballen, Ranigan Walsh, Dr. Michael Felver, Margaret Combs, and Joyce Clateman, as well as the many friends and friends of friends who patiently answered my questions about their own widowhood experiences. There is strength in our mutuality, especially as we all share and recognize this yawning cavity in our hearts that comes from the loss of a loving spouse. And as we help one another to pick ourselves up, one by one, and move on.

Initial comments by my review committee:

Are you serious? I'd hardly call you a lousy widow. Look what you've done in these sad months: more than some people do in five years. All your activities are difficult projects for anyone and you've had the spirit and fortitude to tackle them. You're not sitting around hugging your wedding picture and living a hermit's life. You're a role model for widowhood.

Speaking of Widowhood, of course go ahead and do what you have to do to get it published. You know the steps and have worked hard. And this book is needed.

J.C.

AUTHOR'S BIO

Prior to her husband's massive stroke in 2001 and death in 2020, Berenice Kleiman was a principal in the couple's marketing communications' firm, which represented high-tech companies nationwide. She subsequently functioned for almost 20 years as primary caregiver and advocate. During this period, she has also become both an active playwright and author of four books.

To meet Berenice Kleiman and hear her discussion tune into a podcast interview on "At Home Radio":

http://berenicekleiman.com/press/At_Home_Radio_2020-10-21

Made in United States
Orlando, FL
26 August 2022